VOLUME ONE
KANSAS CITY
OUR COLLECTIVE MEMORIES

BRUCE MATHEWS AND STEVE NOLL

**WORDS AND PHOTOGRAPHS BY
BRUCE MATHEWS**

FOREWORD BY JONATHAN KEMPER

**EDITED BY LYNN MACKLE
DESIGNED BY DAVID SPAW**

CITY SCENE COVER ART BY KATHY BARNARD

SELECTED ADDITIONAL TEXT BY GAYLE KRIGEL AND MARK MORALES

PUBLISHED BY DGHFKC BOOKS, LLC.
PRAIRIE VILLAGE, KANSAS

VOLUME ONE
KANSAS CITY
OUR COLLECTIVE MEMORIES

By Bruce Mathews and Steve Noll

Editor: Lynn Mackle

Designer: David Spaw

ABOUT THE COVER

City Scene created by Kathy Barnard

ISBN: 978-1-943338-09-2

Library of Congress Control Number: 2016950555

First Edition, First Printing

Printed in the United States of America

by Walsworth Publishing Company, Marceline, Missouri

Published by DGHFKC Books, LLC

with assistance provided by publisher Doug Weaver,

Chandler Lake Books, Traverse City, Michigan

DGHFKC, LLC

P. O. Box 8142

Prairie Village, KS 66208

To order copies, call 913-262-1560

Or go to www.historickc.org

DEDICATION

This book is dedicated to the people who have collectively built Kansas City: its neighborhoods, businesses, government institutions, recreational facilities, and cultural venues. We are the grateful recipients of their efforts.

Our treasured artifacts, images, and mementos remind us of our legacy. We appreciate each of the individuals and organizations who have shared their collections and made crafting this book an honor and a privilege.

STEVE NOLL

Acknowledgments

THE PUBLISHERS WOULD LIKE TO EXPRESS THEIR APPRECIATION TO EVERYONE INVOLVED IN MAKING *KANSAS CITY: OUR COLLECTIVE MEMORIES* POSSIBLE.

THE PRODUCTION TEAM

Thanks are due to David Spaw for his superb design and attention to every aspect of the creative process. Lynn Mackle, is appreciated for her editing and meticulous attention to the written word. Stained glass artist Kathy Barnard, for her beautiful sand carved *City Scene* shown on the cover. Publisher Doug Weaver, for his support and guidance throughout the publishing process. Walsworth Publishing Company is to be thanked for excellence in printing, customer service and for demonstrating that such professionals can flourish right here in the Heartland of America. Melanie Mathews is deeply appreciated for her thoughtful insight while reviewing the draft text.

THE CONTRIBUTORS

To all of the individuals and families who so willingly shared their collective treasures: Theresa Andrews; Bob Bernstein; Bruce Bettinger; Michael Bushnell; Tony Cecena, Jr.; Gene Chavez; Nancy and John Dillingham; Daniel DiSalvo, Jr.; Gloria Dobbs and Courtney Sloan; Nancy Finley; Neal Foster; Anita and Gerald Gorman; Shirley and Barnett Helzberg; John Herbst; Pat Jacobs; Dot Johnson; Beth Leibling; Nina Kanaga; Charlotte and Stephen Kirk; Gayle and Bruce Krigel; Nadine and Glenn Kubis; Felicia Londre; John Martin; Melanie and Bruce Mathews; Deanna Mathews; Mike Mathews; Patricia Cleary Miller; Jerry Morales; Mark Morales; Willie and Larry Morgan; Jeri & Bill Murphy; Marianne and Steve Noll; Karol O'Brien; Dorri Partain; Nancy Parton; Janet and Dick Rees; Nancy and Philip Reicher; Steve Reyes; Sally Ruddy; Barbara and Ken Saathoff; The Diego Segui family; Chris Smart; Peggy Smith; Dave Starbuck; Scot Stockton; Mina Steen; Tom Taylor; Abigail and Fred Tempel; Patty and Nick Vedros; Chris Wilborn; John B. Wornall, IV.

To all of the companies, public entities, libraries and museums who opened their archives and hearts that their treasures might be included: City Union Mission; Guadalupe Centers, Inc.; the Hispanic Heritage Baseball Museum Hall of Fame; The Jackson County Historical Society; The Kansas City Star; the Kansas City Baseball Historical Society; the Kansas City Museum; the Kansas City Public Library; the Loose Mansion; the National World War I Museum; the Negro Leagues Museum; the Northeast News; Tension Envelope Corporation; the Harry S. Truman Library and Museum; the TWA Museum; the Westport Historical Society; The John Wornall House Museum.

BRUCE MATHEWS and STEVE NOLL

FOREWORD

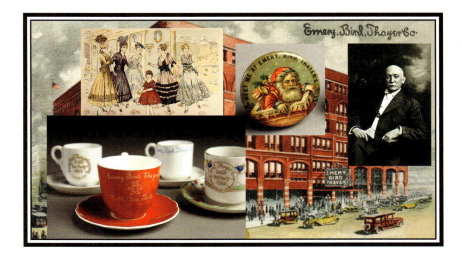

Kansas City: Our Collective Memories is a book that will no doubt have great natural appeal to collectors with any interest in Kansas City's rich legacy of stories and its material culture. These are those who—with varying degrees of passion sometimes approaching gentle madness—collect antiques, souvenirs, ephemera, totems, historical memorabilia, trophies and assorted other keepsakes associated with our town's rich experiences, arts and aspirations.

But I expect that it might also have interest to the many among us who have chosen to pass their days unencumbered by these things which, in their hunt, capture, presentation and conservation, cause the first group such delight. With this delightful book, we can all together experience many of our community's stories afresh, dipping into pages graphically embellished with illustrations of materials which, intentionally or unintentionally, have survived to be enjoyed, treasured and now shared.

Bruce Mathews and Steve Noll have clearly had a lot of fun marshalling their material and producing this most eclectic collection of stories about collections, collectors, and collecting. Their book is a celebration made up of stories told with places and objects saved from oblivion. In a time which is increasingly digital and "virtual," this celebration of things tangible is itself a treasure, and we are all richer for their work in bringing this together in such an attractive and readable form.

JONATHAN KEMPER

TABLE OF CONTENTS

DEDICATION iii

ACKNOWLEDGMENTS iv

FOREWORD v

INTRODUCTION vii

CHAPTER 1: UNIQUELY KANSAS CITY 2
Souvenirs: Plates and Bowls, Public Ceremonies,
Promotion Collectibles, Paperweights, Bottles,
One-of-a-Kind Finds

CHAPTER 2: COMMERCE AND INDUSTRY 26
Retail, Industry, Railroads, Cattle, Wheat, Airlines, Steel,
Garment, Automotive
    Biscuits and Crackers
    Emery, Bird, Thayer Dry Goods Co.
    TWA: Kansas City's Hometown Airline

CHAPTER 3: HOSPITALITY 50
Lodging and Dining
    Hotel Baltimore
    Hotel Muehlebach
    The Golden Ox Restaurant
    The Happy Meal: Born in Kansas City

CHAPTER 4: PUBLIC SPACES 82
Parks, Union Station, Liberty Memorial, Monuments, Fountains
    The Liberty Memorial: Dedications, Rededications, and
    Official Ceremonies

CHAPTER 5: ARTS, ENTERTAINMENT, AND SPORTS 100
Theatres, Amusement Parks, Jazz, Performing Arts, Sports
    Municipal Stadium: The Blues, Monarchs, and A's
    Latino Baseball and Fast-Pitch Softball
    The Golden Gloves: A Tribute to Jerry Morales
    Priests of Pallas

CHAPTER 6: POLITICS 138
Political Conventions, Local Elections, Harry Truman, Politicians
    Kansas City's National Political Conventions

CHAPTER 7: TIMES OF TRIAL 148

Wars, Civil Rights, Suffrage, Hunger, Poverty, Social Activism
Lt. Frederic Herbert Olander Jr., POW - WWII
Pvt. Daniel DiSalvo Sr. - WWII
God's Human Sparrows: The Story of City Union Mission

CHAPTER 8: EDUCATION 164

Public Schools, Libraries, Higher Education
The Kansas City Public Library: The Early Years

CHAPTER 9: FAMILY TREASURES 174

Heirlooms, Furniture, Photographs
Harry Truman: On a Personal Note
The Proposal: The Marriage of John B. Wornall and Eliza Johnson
The Krigel Family History Table
Sally, Family, and Friends
Hattie's Rocking Chair
The Kubis Family Photos

THE PUBLISHING TEAM. 216

BIBLIOGRAPHY 218
INDEX 221

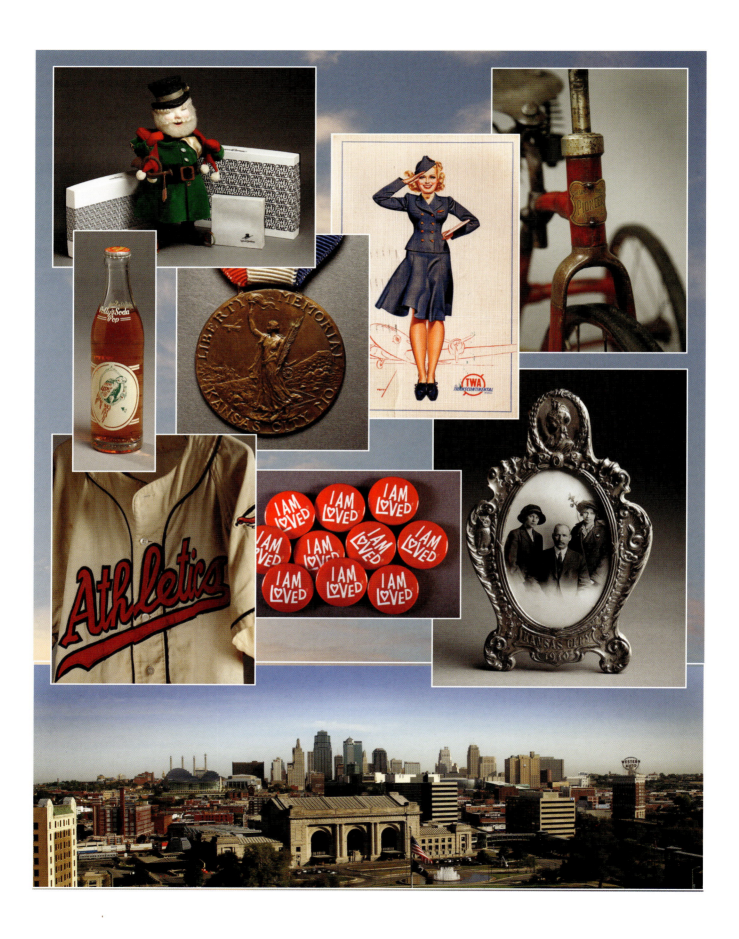

INTRODUCTION

Throughout our lives we collect things—things we care about. These collections may start with a first doll, or a baseball glove from our childhood. What we collect satisfies our need to simply hold on to something. Our collections, in their own way, become comfort food for the heart and mind. Whether the collection consists of books or friendships, they become our cherished memories and our link to the past.

As a community, our collections reveal what makes us proud of where we live and the people we live with, as well as those who came before us. Adele Hall often referred to "our ancestors on whose shoulders we stand today." A simple postcard is a glimpse into the lives of those who are generations removed. We see the streets where they lived, the appearance of their homes, and how they dressed. Hats, for example, take us back to a time of grace and elegance. Baseball bats, on the other hand, evoke the pure joy of childhood. The players may change, but the enjoyment of the game never does.

What we collect, as a community, becomes a part of our legacy. These very special items help reveal who we are and where we came from. *Kansas City: Our Collective Memories* takes us on a journey of memories formed by each of us, to be cherished by all of us. There are artifacts from local museums, to be sure. But the vast majority of these collections have come from you, your neighbors, or members of your own family. It was our intent from the beginning to share a glimpse of important treasures that might never be found in a museum. Many are unique, or one-of-a-kind. Some of them bring tears to our eyes. Others make us laugh out loud. They are, after all, the fabric of our community.

Volume One of *Kansas City: Our Collective Memories* is but a start. Additional volumes will reveal more treasures and recall even more memories. Enjoy.

BRUCE MATHEWS

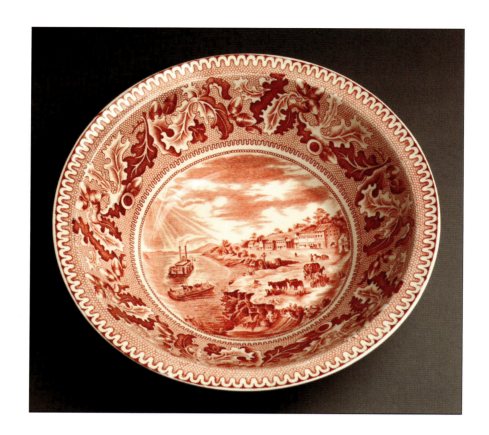

The Town of Kansas, circa 1850, bowl and lithograph
Source, bowl: The Steve Noll Collection
Source, lithograph: Missouri Valley Special Collections,
The Kansas City Public Library

Uniquely Kansas City

In 1821, François Gesseau Chouteau (1797-1838) and his wife, Bérénice Thérèse Ménard (1801-1880), established a trading post and the first permanent European American settlement on a site near the confluence of the Missouri and Kansas rivers. That rudimentary outpost would evolve into the Town of Kansas, which was incorporated on June 1, 1850. By 1853, it boasted a population of sixty-seven, and the citizens had elected their first mayor.

A few houses, commercial businesses, and warehouses stood at the foot of the bluffs in the vicinity of what is now Main Street. A hotel had also been established. Travelers on riverboats needed only to venture a few miles overland to Westport, where outfitters could provide them with goods they needed for the long journey west, via the Santa Fe, California, and Oregon trails.

By 1865, the Civil War had ended. As it grew, the fledgling community spread to the south, and the first bridge to span the Missouri River at any point along its meandering course was completed in 1869. The population exploded, the landscape changed, and the destiny of Kansas City took shape.

Kansas City has been a community of collectors since those early times. We have gathered and archived items that remind us of our ancestors, our childhood days, our past homes, and places we have visited. These "collectibles" form our identity. They connect us with those around us, endowing us with a sense of pride in the place we call home.

SOUVENIRS

Kansas City, Missouri, ashtray, featuring Union Station, Liberty Memorial and J. C. Nichols Fountain
Source: The Steve Noll Collection

"Souvenir of Kansas City, Mo." glass
Silver spoons for: Missouri, Kansas and Kansas City
Source, all: The Dot Johnson Collection

Kansas City Icons – lady's handkerchief featuring:
Municipal Airport, Swope Park Gateway, Municipal Auditorium, Liberty Memorial,
Kansas City, Missouri, skyline, *The Scout* statue, Kersey Coates Drive,
Union Station and *Pioneer Mother* statue
Source: The Gloria Dobbs and Courtney Sloan Collection

PLATES AND BOWLS

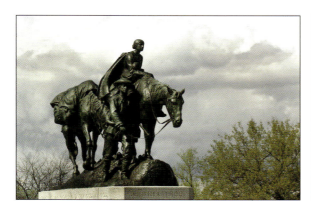 

Left: The Pioneer Mother Memorial in Penn Valley Park
Gifted to Kansas City by William Volker
Right: Kansas City, Missouri, Souvenir Plate
Featuring: *Pioneer Mother*, Liberty Memorial, *The Scout*,
Municipal Airport, Civic Center, Union Station, Municipal Auditorium, and Post Office
Source, bowl: The Steve Noll Collection

Left: Kansas City souvenir plate featuring:
Union Station, Truman Home, Municipal Auditorium, J.C. Nichols Fountain,
Truman Library and Great Ape House at the Kansas City Zoo.
Right: Union Station, 2016
Source: The Steve Noll Collection

In 1832 Col. John Harris and his wife, Henrietta Simpson, migrated from Kentucky to the area known as West Port. Here he became the proprietor of the Harris House Hotel. In 1855 Harris built a grand "Mansion House" for his family. The house was moved to its present location in 1922 and is operated as a historical museum by the Westport Historical Society.

After Col. Harris's death in 1855 their daughter Josephine and her husband, Col. Charles E. Kearney, along with their five children, moved into the home to care for the aging Henrietta. A number of artifacts, including this footed bowl that belonged to Josephine, are on display in what is now referred to as the Harris-Kearney House.

Left: Footed bowl belonging to Josephine (Harris) Kearney
Source: The Westport Historical Society Collection
Right: *Harris House* **by Charles Goslin**
Source: Jackson County Historical Society

Built in 1850 by George and William Ewing, the oldest surviving building in Kansas City stands at the northwestern corner of Westport Road and Pennsylvania Avenue. It is historically noted as the home of the A.G. Boone and Company Trading Post. Albert Gallatin Boone, grandson of frontiersman Daniel Boone, supplied provisions to wagon trains as they began their arduous treks along the trails leading west. Today, the building houses the popular Kelly's Westport Inn, in the heart of Westport's entertainment, dining, and shopping district.

Plate featuring the oldest building in Kansas City and archival photo of the same building
Westport Road and Pennsylvania Avenue
Source: Plate – The Steve Noll Collection
Source: Archival photo - Missouri Valley Special Collections, Kansas City Public Library

PUBLIC CEREMONIES

SWOPE PARK DEDICATION OF 1896

On June 25, 1896, more than 18,000 Kansas Citians ventured to a spot four miles to the south of the city limits. There they would gather in a "Grand Jubilee" to dedicate as a public park more than 1,300 acres and to honor its benefactor, Colonel Thomas Hunton Swope. Col. Swope had come to Kansas City in 1857 as a real estate investor. He soon became the largest landowner in the city. Although himself somewhat of a recluse and an anonymous donor in many instances he became one of the city's most prominent philanthropists. When the day of the jubilee arrived, Col. Swope could be seen walking the grounds and attending to details. But by the time the activities started, he had left the park, leaving local dignitaries and excited citizens to revel in the festivities without him. He gave the park to the city with just three restrictions: "That the land be named Swope Park, that it be used forever as a park and that the city spend a set amount each year for ten years to improve it."

On April 8, 1918, eight-and-a-half years after his mysterious death, Col. Swope was laid to rest in the park. His grave is marked by a large memorial featuring a Greek Temple watched over by a pair of stone lions. Over the years Swope Park has grown to more than 1,800 acres and is home to the Kansas City Zoo, two golf courses, Starlight Theatre, numerous shelter houses and other outdoor sites for the public to enjoy. It is the largest park in Kansas City and is the crown jewel of Kansas City's world-renowned parks and boulevard system.

  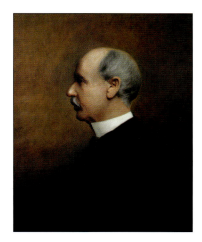

Commemorative medallion from the dedication of Swope Park
"All Honor to Thomas H. Swope"
June 25, 1896
Source: The Anita Gorman Collection

Ribbon worn by all attending the dedication of Swope Park
"In Honor of Kansas City's Friend and Benefactor – Thomas H. Swope"
Source: Missouri Valley Special Collections, Kansas City Public Library

Portrait of Col. Thomas H. Swope, benefactor of Swope Park
Source: Kansas City, Missouri, Parks and Recreation

Gravesite of Col. Thomas Hunton Swope, located in the
beautiful public park that bears his name

Early postcard view of the Shelter House near the main entrance to Swope Park
Source: The Tom Taylor Collection

BATTLE OF WESTPORT
125th ANNIVERSARY REENACTMENT IN 1989

The Battle of Westport, often referred to as the "Gettysburg of the West," was waged on October 21-23, 1864. The total of 30,000 soldiers who participated in a series of battles over the three days pitted forces under Confederate General Sterling Price against those of Union General Samuel Curtis. The battle brought on by the Confederates was intended to force the Union to send more troops to the Western theatre of the war, thus relieving pressure on the Rebel army in the east. On the last day, however, Union forces under General Alfred Pleasanton made a strong showing at Byram's Ford and Price's army retreated south from what is now the Country Club Plaza and Loose Park.

While it might have been heralded as the "Gettysburg of the West," it was not a turning point in the war. It was another sign of the beginning of the end for the beleaguered Confederate army.

In 1989 reenactors gathered near the Byram's Ford site, in Swope Park, actually, to commemorate the 125th anniversary of the battle. They gathered again in 2014 to mark the 150th anniversary. Today the scattered battlefield sites are listed on the National Register of Historic Places. There are markers at the various locations, including an interpretative site on the south lawn of Loose Park.

The Battle of Westport - 1864, **by N. C. Wyeth**
Source: Missouri Valley Special Collections, Kansas City Public Library

Left: Commemorative belt buckle from 1989 Reenactment
Source: Westport Historical Society
Right: Reenactment ticket and anniversary medallion
Source: The Anita Gorman Collection

Battle of Westport interpretative site in Loose Park

THE KANSAS CITY, MISSOURI, CENTENNIAL 1850 – 1950

Kansas City Centennial souvenir program
Source: The Michael Bushnell Collection

Left: U.S. postage stamp commemorating the Kansas City, Missouri, Centennial
Source: The Bruce Mathews Collection
Right: June 3, 1950, First Day of Issue envelope
Source: The Steve Noll Collection

Centennial historic building glasses featuring (left to right):
Grand Central Station, City Hall, Main Street circa 1868,
First Convention Hall, Federal Post Office and Custom House
Source: The Steve Noll Collection

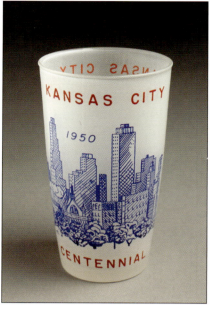

Centennial cup and glasses
Source: The Steve Noll Collection

Kansas City Centennial commemorative coin
Left, front side: Kansas City Centennial 1850-1950
Right, reverse side: American Royal Live Stock and Horse Show October 14-21, 1950.
Best Wishes Nelly Don, Saddle and Sirloin Club,
Operation New Orleans – April 1950
Source: The Steve Noll Collection

KANSAS CITY INTERNATIONAL AIRPORT DEDICATION – 1972

In October of 1972, the 10,000-acre airport complex in Platte County, Missouri, was dedicated and officially became Kansas City International Airport. The new KCI, located some fifteen miles north of downtown Kansas City, replaced Kansas City's aging and landlocked Municipal Airport just north across the Missouri River adjacent to downtown. Municipal Airport remains an active airport, accommodating smaller planes requiring shorter runways. It has been renamed the Charles B. Wheeler Downtown Airport. Both airports are operated by the Kansas City, Missouri, Aviation Department. For years the airport complex in Platte County had been known as Mid-Continent International Airport. It served as the landing strip for the Trans World Airlines (TWA) overhaul base. With the name change to KCI, three separate terminal buildings, designed by the architectural firm of Kivett & Myers, were constructed to accommodate the increased traffic.

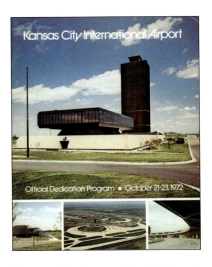

Kansas City International Airport
dedication program - October 21-23, 1972
Source: The Michael Bushnell Collection

KCI dedicatory medallion
Source: The Anita Gorman Collection

THE CHILDREN'S FOUNTAIN DEDICATION – 1995

The Children's Fountain is located at the intersection of North Oak Street Trafficway and Northeast Thirty-second Avenue in North Kansas City, Missouri. Dedicated on June 21, 1995, the fountain was made possible by a four-year fundraising effort led by Northland resident Anita Gorman, during her tenure as president of the Kansas City, Missouri, Parks and Recreation Board. Designed by sculptor Tom Corbin, the fountain features six bronze statues of children at play. The dedicatory plaque reads: "The bronze figures represent children everywhere to whom this fountain is dedicated and the activities that shape young lives, making childhood a joy." The fountain and landscaped grounds are located on property donated by the Missouri Department of Highways and Transportation.

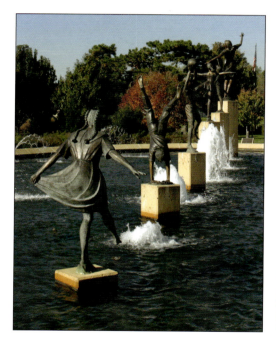 

The Children's Fountain dedicatory souvenir
Source: The Anita Gorman Collection

PROMOTION COLLECTIBLES

Commerce Trust Company

The Commerce Trust Company building was constructed in 1907 at Tenth and Walnut in downtown Kansas City. Commerce Trust had originally been formed in April 1865, immediately after the Civil War, as the Kansas City Savings Association. Dr. William Stone Woods bought the controlling interest in the bank in 1881 and became its president. The sixteen-story building has seen many changes over the years but has remained the home of Commerce Trust Company for more than a century.

Left: Commerce Trust Company money clip
Source: The Gloria Dobbs Collection
Right: Archival photo of Commerce Trust Company building, circa 1935
Source: The Chris Wilborn Collection

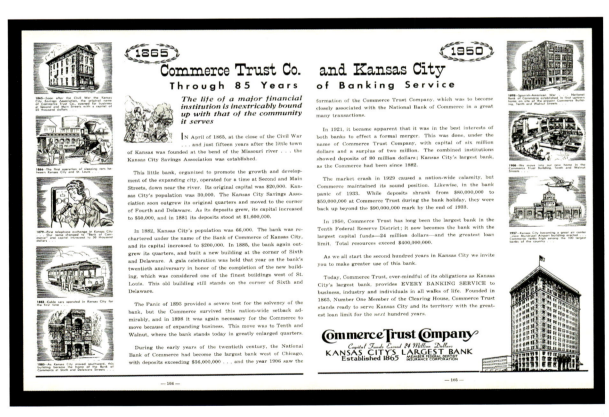

**Commerce Trust Company advertisement in the
Kansas City Centennial program**
Source: The Michael Bushnell Collection

HELZBERG DIAMONDS

The "I Am Loved" button has been an advertising trademark for Helzberg Diamonds since 1967. Barnett Helzberg first sketched the phrase after his love, Shirley Bush, accepted his proposal of marriage. More than fifty million buttons have since been produced in eleven languages. Even after Warren Buffet's 1995 purchase of the company, the "I Am Loved" button remains an icon.

Helzberg Diamonds "I Am Loved" buttons
Source: The Shirley and Barnett Helzberg Collection

DECOURSEY'S CREAMERY COMPANY

The first James H. DeCoursey showed an adventurous spirit as a young Forty-niner, seeking his fortune in the gold mines of California. DeCoursey returned to his native Kansas after his mining days, purchasing land there before setting off to fight in the Civil War. When the war ended, the rugged entrepreneur, who was one of the Midwest's first door-to-door milkmen, proceeded to found a commercial creamery bearing his name. The DeCoursey Creamery Company grew into a family-operated venture run by generations of the DeCoursey clan.

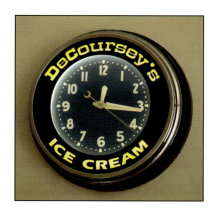

DeCoursey's Ice Cream clock
Source: The Patty and Nick Vedros Collection

UNITY VEGETARIAN INN AND CAFETERIA

The Unity Inn was opened on the first floor of a two-story frame house at 913 Tracy Street in 1906. The brainchild of Unity Village founders Charles and Myrtle Fillmore, it was the first all-vegetarian eatery in Kansas City. In a 2012 article in The Pitch, Charles Ferruzza wrote: "The restaurant opened with meatless cuisine and good intentions. Perhaps their intentions were too good. During the opening weeks of the inn, patrons could pay as little or as much for their meals as they wished. It was a noble gesture, but the Fillmores sadly learned that some people in this city didn't understand the real meaning of the word gratitude."

Local author and historian Tom Taylor writes in his 2009 book, *Unity Village*: "Workers in the restaurant handed out cards that read, 'All the expenses of this house are met by the freewill offering of its guests. Freely you have received, freely give.' "

Shortly after the restaurant opened, before it would surely have become bankrupt, Taylor writes: "The staff started charging set prices for modest meals. It became so successful that by the start of World War II, the Unity Inn was one of the largest vegetarian venues in the United States, sometimes serving as many as 10,000 meals a week. Finally, when Unity Village was opened in 1949 in Lee's Summit, the inn was relocated there." At the time this book was published in 2016, the original building at Ninth Street and Tracy was still standing.

Unity Vegetarian Inn and Cafeteria
Ninth and Tracy, Kansas City, Missouri
Source: Phonograph Record: The Steve Noll Collection
Source: Archival Photographs: Missouri Valley Special Collections,
Kansas City Public Library

MATCHBOOKS

Not that long ago, matchbooks and ashtrays were utilized as a major form of advertising for local businesses. At their peak, they became highly desirable collectibles. As the sampling below indicates, matchbooks could be found as an advertising medium not only for restaurants, but also for clothing stores, industrial supply businesses, diaper service companies, bowling alleys, car washes and auto repair shops, just to name a few. It is especially interesting to note advertisements such as one promoting Trans World Airlines. That particular ad shows couples dining in high style, while enjoying their favorite cigarettes. Ashtrays, built into the arms of seats, were a common sight to accommodate even first-class flyers.

Matchbook covers advertising bowling alleys, car washes, clothing stores, flying lessons, a diaper service company, banks… You name it!
Source: The Theresa Andrews Collection

Restaurant matchbooks:
Eddy's, Putsch's 210, Stephenson's, Italian Gardens, Las Palmas, Mancusso's, Roselli's, Carousel Cafeteria, Southern Mansion and The Flying Chicken, among others
Source: The Theresa Andrews Collection

PAPERWEIGHTS

The second Jackson County Courthouse was completed in 1892, at the cost of $500,000. It was located in the block near City Market, bounded by Missouri, Fifth, Oak, and Locust streets. The building was utilized for more than forty-three years, until the present courthouse was completed in 1934.

Left: Archival photo of 1892 Jackson County Courthouse
Source: The Kansas City Museum Collection
Right: Jackson County Courthouse paperweight
Source: The Steve Noll Collection

Kansas City's massive City Hall was completed in 1893. It stood proudly on the eastern side of Main Street, between Fourth and Fifth streets. It housed various city departments, including the chambers of the city council, the police department, courts, and jail. The city's health department was also located within its walls. The landscaped garden area shown in the photograph eventually gave way to the construction of an annex building. The structure was razed when the present-day City Hall, located in the block extending from Eleventh Street to Twelfth Street and Oak Street to Locust Street, was completed.

Left: Kansas City's City Hall paperweight
Source: The Steve Noll Collection
Right: Archival photograph of 1893 City Hall
Source: The Kansas City Museum Collection

The Daily Drovers Telegram was founded in 1881 by Jay Holcomb Neff to report on the Kansas City Stockyards and livestock business. Eventually the paper was purchased by Vance Publishing and became known as the Kansas City Daily Drovers Telegram. Neff would be elected as Mayor of Kansas City and served in 1904-05.

 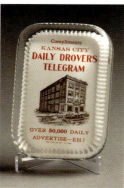

Left: Archival photo of the Kansas City Daily Drovers Telegram building
Source: Missouri Valley Special Collections, Kansas City Public Library
Right: Daily Drovers Daily Telegram paperweight
Source, paperweight: The Steve Noll Collection

BOTTLES

In 1923, the original Polly's Soda Pop was taken over by Louis and Dorothea Compton in Independence, Missouri. It sold for five cents a bottle. The company ceased operations in 1967, after a successful run of more than fifty years.

  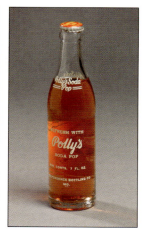

Polly's Soda Pop bottles
Source: The Dick Rees Collection

**Archival photograph of Independence Bottling Company,
the home of Polly's Soda Pop**
Source: Missouri Valley Special Collections, Kansas City Public Library

Originally formed as the Faxon, Horton & Gallagher Drug Company, this Kansas City-based wholesale drug company boasted clients in each of the western states. James Horton, a Kansas state senator, retired from the business in 1906. Frank Faxon and John A. Gallagher purchased Horton's shares and continued to manufacture a large inventory of products, including toiletries, face creams, and perfumes. The company was highly successful. Frank Faxon was a man known for his commitment "to make Kansas City a good place to live in." He served on the city council, co-founded the Commercial Club, and worked tirelessly for better conditions in schools and workplaces throughout Kansas City. At the time of his death in 1912, Faxon served as president of the Kansas City Board of Education.

Faxon & Gallagher Drug Company bottle
Source: The Bruce Bettinger Collection

FAXON & GALLAGHER DRUG CO.

WHOLESALE DRUGGISTS

DRUGGISTS SUNDRIES

N. W. Cor. 8th and Broadway   Kansas City, Mo.

Faxon & Gallagher Drug Company advertisement
Source: "Kansas City: Its Resources and Their Development"
from Missouri Valley Special Collections, Kansas City Public Library

Kansas City's Thomas J. "Boss Tom" Pendergast made his early money in the importing and distributing of liquor that included White Horse Whisky. Pendergast controlled the city's corrupt political machine during the 1920s and 1930s, which eventually resulted in his conviction for tax fraud. Pendergast spent fifteen months in the penitentiary at Fort Leavenworth, Kansas.

White Horse Whisky was a blended whisky that was shipped to wholesalers in the United States from Glasgow, Scotland. It was the favorite of Jackie Gleason's character "Minnesota Fats," who appeared in the 1961 classic, *The Hustler*.

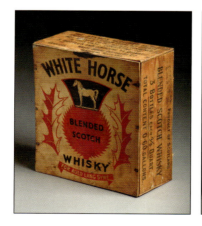 

T. J. Pendergast Wholesale Liquor Company shipping container
for White Horse Blended Scotch Whisky
Source: The Bruce Bettinger Collection

ONE-OF-A-KIND FINDS

Young August Hummel immigrated to Kansas City in 1901 from the Black Forest region of Germany. He brought with him the skills he had learned as a brass finisher and machinist in his homeland. For more than a century, four generations of the family have been operating what began as Acme Brass Machine Works. Today, the business is known as Acme Brass Custom Plating. Times have changed since the company was formed as a brass foundry and manufacturing business. It now offers a wide range of services, ranging from fabricating custom hardware to refinishing antique fixtures. The company works with architects and designers to blend old-world traditions with state-of-the-art technology.

Candlestick holders (left) and door knocker (right)
created by August Karl Hummel for the family home
3925 Holmes – Kansas City, Missouri
Source: The Karol O'Brien Collection

H. Roe Bartle can be described as a true larger-than-life character. Possessed of impressive physical stature, he was charismatic and could sell almost anything. Bartle was involved in Scouting for most of his life. He served as executive of the Kansas City Area Council for the Boy Scouts. He established the "Tribe of Mic-O-Say," where he was affectionately known as "The Chief." He was elected mayor of Kansas City and served two terms, from 1956 to 1963. While mayor, he played a critical role in the decision of Dallas Texans owner Lamar Hunt to relocate his professional football team to Kansas City. The team was renamed the Kansas City Chiefs in Bartle's honor.

Clinton W. Kanaga served as a Second Lieutenant in the United States Marine Corps during World War II. In Kansas City he served as a member of the Board of Police Commissioners by appointment of both Governors John Dalton and Joe Teasdale. He was also appointed by Governor Warren Hearnes to serve as Chairman of the Kansas City Area Transportation Authority. He was a personal friend of Mayor H. Roe Bartle. As Bartle chuckled in this caricature of the two he credited Kanaga with making him the "Lord Mayor" of America's greatest city.

Artist Jack O'Hara was nationally known for his work, primarily as a watercolorist. As such, he achieved membership in the American Watercolor Society. O'Hara's paintings are exhibited in permanent collections in numerous museums, including the Nelson-Atkins Museum of Art; the Spencer Museum of the University of Kansas; the Albrecht-Kemper Museum in St. Joseph, Missouri; the Farnsworth Museum in Rockland, Maine; the Muchnic Art Gallery in Atchison, Kansas; the Kansas City Art Institute; and the Nevada Museum of Art in Reno, Nevada. After serving in World War II, O'Hara was employed by Hallmark Cards. For some twenty-one years, he was a partner with the Valentine-Radford Advertising Agency. O'Hara spent his later years as a full-time artist.

**Pen and ink drawing of Mayor H. Roe Bartle and
his friend Clinton Kanaga by Kansas City artist Jack O'Hara**

*"To my very dear friend who made me the Lord Mayor
of America's greatest City, Clint, with affectionate regards.
Always your pal, H. Roe Bartle 'Chief'"*
Source: The Nina Kanaga Collection

Inscribed upon an important Dillingham family heirloom are these words: "Jay Dillingham, president of the Kansas City Stockyards Co., gets a 'Key to the City' as well as a hearty handshake from Mayor H. Roe Bartle in recognition of his long and stellar service to the community. Dillingham, who is past president of both the Chamber of Commerce and the American Royal Livestock and Horse Show, holds the tie-clasp key in his free hand. Ceremonies took place at the annual banquet of the International Brangus Breeders Association in Kansas City, at which Mayor Bartle was the featured speaker."

Key to the City presented to Jay Dillingham by Kansas City, Missouri, Mayor H. Roe Bartle, April 1962
Source: The John Dillingham Collection

Sunshine Krispy Cracker Tin
Source: The Ken and Barbara Saathoff Collection

In 1905, Jacob and his company were responsible for inventing the Hydrox Cookie. In 1917, they invented the soda cracker. The Hi-Ho and Krispy Crackers trace their origin back to those early days of the company.

– Ken Saathoff

BISCUITS AND CRACKERS

Jacob Leander Loose
Source: The Nancy Parton Collection

When you hear the name "Loose" in Kansas City, you likely think of the lovely eighty-acre park just south of the famed Country Club Plaza shopping district. Alternatively, the magnificent Loose Mansion at 101 East Armour Boulevard may spring to mind. Perhaps you will reflect upon the many philanthropic accomplishments of the Loose family, wondering how the family's wealth was acquired. Remarkably, the story began with biscuits and crackers.

The best-known couple in the Loose clan was surely Jacob Leander Loose and his wife, Ella Anna Clark. Jacob was a highly successful businessman in his own right; but after his death, his beloved wife did everything in her power to perpetuate her husband's name and legacy. The couple was not born wealthy, but fortune certainly smiled upon them. Two inscribed family photographs help place events into perspective. The first shows Ella as a young girl prior to her marriage, dressed in a pretty, but simple, dress. The

"Ella, before money"   **"Ella, after money"**
Source, both: The Nancy Parton Collection

words "Ella, before money" are penned on the photo's reverse side. The second photograph captures Ella shortly after her marriage, wearing an elaborate gown enhanced with elegant accessories. The inscription on the back of this one reads, "Ella, after money." And so it was.

The saga of the Loose family's successful business ventures began in 1885, when Jacob Loose purchased the Corie Cracker and Confectionery Company in partnership with his brother Joseph. A commanding figure, Jacob would take the reins in running the growing enterprises, which he served as president. The entrepreneurs soon changed the organization's name to Loose Brothers Manufacturing Company. Five years later, they renamed it the American Biscuit Company. By 1899 the company's holdings had grown to seventeen regional bakeries, which were scattered throughout the country. The next step was a merger with the National Biscuit Company (Nabisco). In 1902, the brothers left Nabisco to form a new venture, the Loose-Wiles Biscuit Company, which sold products under the brand name of Sunshine Biscuits. By 1930, the company boasted 30,000 employees, including 1,500 salesmen. Jacob Loose ultimately changed the company's name to the now-familiar moniker of Sunshine Biscuits. (It was no coincidence that "Sunshine" was his wife's nickname.)

Ken and Barbara Saathoff, current owners of the Loose Mansion, offer this insight into the company's success: "In 1905, Jacob and his company were responsible for inventing the Hydrox Cookie. In 1917, they invented the soda cracker. The ever-popular Hi-Ho and Krispy Crackers trace their origin back to those early days of the company, which also sold candy and

Loose-Wiles / Sunshine Biscuit tins

Left: Sunshine Fruit Cake Tin / Right: Square Biscuit Type "C" – World War I

Left: Toy Sunshine Biscuit Truck
Right: Merchant's scale for weighing Loose-Wiles products, such as candy and cookies

Advertisement for Sunshine
Tak-hom-a Biscuit

Source, all: The Ken and Barbara Saathoff Collection

 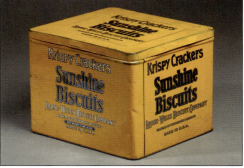

Left: Loose-Wiles Pure Sugar Stick Candy postcard / Right: Krispy Crackers – Sunshine Biscuits tin
Source, both: The Steve Noll Collection

Left: The Loose-Wiles – Sunshine Biscuit Bakery / Right: Loose-Wiles Biscuit Co. delivery truck
Source: Missouri Valley Special Collections, Kansas City Public Library

chocolates. One reason the company was so successful was their creative packaging and advertising." Loose-Wiles and Sunshine artifacts are highly collectible today. Thanks to the Saathoffs, a number of these items are now on display for guests who attend the many special events held in the mansion, which is now available for private gatherings.

The four-story Loose Mansion is listed on the National Register of Historic Places. Constructed between 1907 and 1909, it has been meticulously restored to its former glory. Included within its walls are twelve bathrooms and twelve balconies. Eight of the original eleven fireplaces remain. Together with the carriage house the mansion comprises 17,000 square feet. The home features a large marble entry, a "Grand Salon," a dining room with its own Tiffany chandelier, and a music room complete with a performance stage. Cigar and billiard rooms welcome guests on the lower level. According to Ken, "The wood on the main level is of hand-carved Philippine Mahogany. The sun porch has its original imported Italian tile floor." The sun porch also boasts a Bible fireplace created in tile by the artist Henry Chapin Mercer.

The Loose Mansion, 101 East Armour Boulevard, Kansas City, Missouri

The Entry   Two of the eight fireplaces   The Grand Staircase

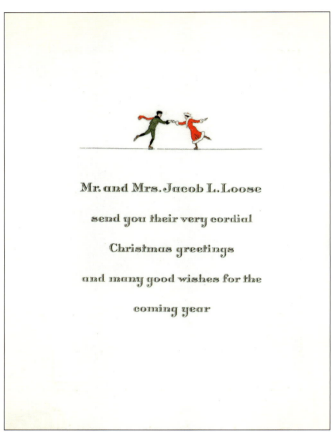

Christmas card
"Mr. and Mrs. Jacob L. Loose send you … for the coming year."
Source: Missouri Valley Special Collections, Kansas City Public Library

The Looses were generous benefactors of the city's many charities. The combined estates of Jacob and Joseph Loose were crucial in the early years of the Greater Kansas City Community Foundation and Affiliated Trusts. After Jacob's death in 1923, Ella continued her philanthropic endeavors for another twenty-two years before her own demise in 1945. Perhaps motivated by the loss of her own two children in their infancies, Ella was especially fond of children's charities. She will be remembered for her Christmas presents of shoes given to the needy children at the Gillis Home in Kansas City. Children's Mercy Hospital also benefited from her bequest.

Ella began a personal crusade to ensure that her husband's name would live on after his passing. As part of that mission, she acquired an eighty-acre tract of land from the Kansas City Country Club and donated it the city for the creation of the Jacob L. Loose Memorial Park. To think, it all began with biscuits and crackers….

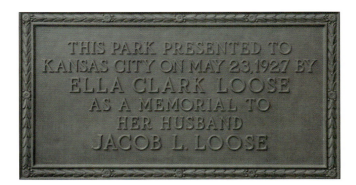

Entrance sign to Loose Park, Wornall Road at Fifty-first Street

Jacob L. Loose Memorial Statue at Loose Park
Presented to Kansas City by Ella Clark Loose in cherished memory of her husband

Loose Lake   The Laura Conyers Smith Municipal Rose Garden

Reception Toilette in Black Velvet, from 1896 Coming Styles catalog
Emery, Bird, Thayer Dry Goods Company
Source: The Neal Foster Collection

EMERY, BIRD, THAYER DRY GOODS CO.

Early rendering of Bullene, Moore & Emery store
Source: The Neal Foster Collection

Postcard view of Petticoat Lane showing EBT on the right
Source: The Steve Noll Collection

The names associated with the iconic Emery, Bird, Thayer Dry Goods Company changed as frequently as the partners in an ever-evolving law firm.

The original store stood at the corner of Main Street and Missouri Street, in downtown Kansas City. When it entered the mercantile world in 1863, the fledgling concern bore the names of its first two partners, Col. Kersey Coates and William Gillis. Both entrepreneurs went on to become principals in an array of other enterprises. Gillis ultimately sold his share to Lathrop Bullene of Leavenworth, Kansas, who changed the company's name from Coates & Gillis to Coates & Bullene. When Coates sold his own interest to Lathrop Bullene's brother Thomas, the company acquired the moniker of Bullene & Brother.

After struggling through the hardships brought on by the Civil War, the store rebounded, along with the economy of Kansas City. In 1867, W. E. Emery was welcomed into the store's ownership group, followed by L. T. Moore in 1870. The new and prosperous concern, which had relocated into larger quarters at the corner of Seventh Street and Delaware Avenue, acquired the name of Bullene, Moore, Emery & Company.

Joseph Taylor Bird, his wife, Annie, and their Valentine neighborhood home, "Elmhurst"
Source: Missouri Valley Special Collections, Kansas City Public Library

Joseph Taylor Bird came on board in 1881, and William Bridges Thayer joined the firm in 1884. After the death of Thomas Bullene, the three remaining partners took the helm. Porter T. Hall, son-in-law of Joseph T. Bird, rose from the store's lower ranks to become president and general manager. The entire cast of family members would enjoy continued success under the name that stuck, one recognizable to Kansas Citians and shoppers around the country: the Emery, Bird, Thayer Dry Goods Company. Usually known simply as EBT, the store soon became an integral part of the fabric of the community.

By the late 1880s, the thriving business had made its move to a new, six-story structure encompassing the southern portion of the block bounded by Tenth Street and Eleventh Street and Grand Avenue and Walnut Street. Kansas Citians dubbed the area "Petticoat Lane." Henry Van Brunt, of the nationally recognized local architectural firm of Van Brunt & Howe, designed the stately structure. Van Brunt chose the "Free Romanesque" style for his masterpiece, which boasted clusters of handsome columns. The arcade that ran its entire length became a popular gathering place for throngs of window shoppers seeking shelter from the elements.

Teacups from doll tea parties   **Santa Claus pins**
Source: The Neal Foster Collection

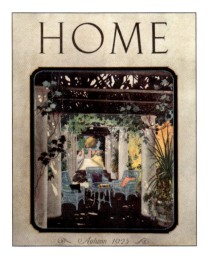 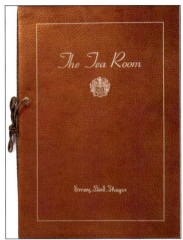

Left: EBT Home Catalog, 1923   **Right: EBT Tea Room Menu**
Source, both: The Neal Foster Collection

Cup from 1914 doll tea party   **Hat and shopping bag from EBT**
Source: The Neal Foster Collection   *Source: The Gloria Dobbs and Courtney Sloan Collection*

Paris styles 1916
Source, all: The Neal Foster Collection

EBT was much more than a mere store: it functioned as an elegant event space. Practically anything the discriminating shopper's heart desired existed within its six stories, from Parisian fashions to the latest toys. The third-floor tearoom became a favored dining venue, and the "doll tea parties" featured prominently on the holiday social scene. These fêtes attracted as many as 5,000 little girls during their one-weekend-a-year runs. As might be expected, patrons habitually flocked to the classic soda fountain.

EBT's vast floor space delighted shoppers. Renovators later removed 70,000 yards of carpeting to reveal hardwood flooring that exuded warmth and character, but creaked with every step. Other memorable features included the manually operated elevators and the bank of clocks located above them on the first floor.

**The American Flag covers the Grand Avenue façade of EBT
as thousands of patriotic Kansas Citians celebrate the end of World War I.**
Source: The Chris Wilborn Collection

To the dismay of its loyal patrons, the shopping paradise could not with-stand the advent of the automobile and the suburban shopping mall. At the end of World War II, Scruggs-Vandervoort-Barney of St. Louis purchased EBT from the remaining family members. The store continued operations until 1967, when it could no longer compete with the impersonal galleries that had replaced it. Gone were the all-day shopping, dining and social experiences that characterized EBT. An entire era had ended. Although the building took its place on the National Register of Historic Places, it, too, gave way to the wrecking ball in 1970. United Missouri Bank, an architec-tural gem in its own right, occupies the store's former site. Time marches on, but memories remain. Thankfully, sentimental souls keep the memo-ries alive with the treasured keepsakes they have collected and maintained throughout the decades.

Elevator, stained glass, and architectural stonework from
Emery, Bird, Thayer Dry Goods Company
Most recently from the EBT Restaurant, I-435 and State Line, Kansas City (now closed)

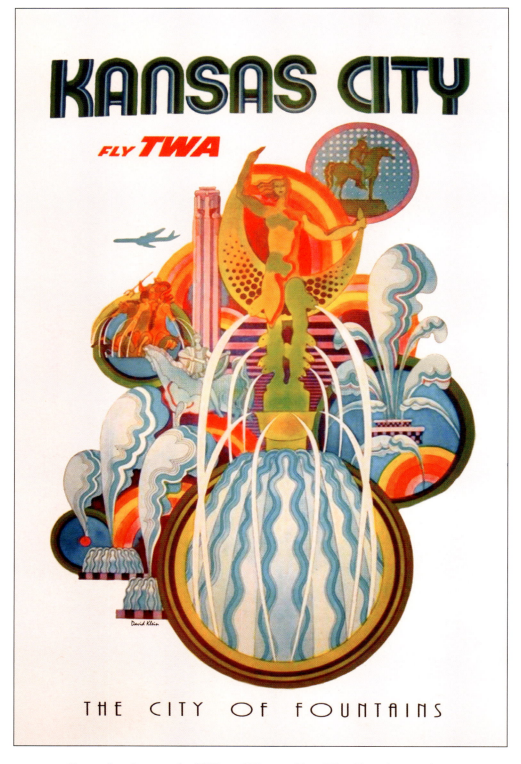

Promotional poster for TWA and Kansas City, "The City of Fountains"
Source: The Dick Rees Collection

KANSAS CITY'S HOMETOWN AIRLINE

TRANS WORLD AIRLINES

The highly recognizable TWA "Twin Globe" logo
Source: The TWA Museum, Charles B. Wheeler Downtown Airport, Kansas City, Missouri

The relationship between Kansas City and TWA was always a love affair, although at times the affair was one-sided. In 2001, when the TWA logo was removed from the massive overhaul base, the city felt as jilted as though she had been scorned by an out-of-town lover who was only in the relationship for her inheritance. TWA's departure from the city brought an end to an economic force and major employer within the city. At its peak TWA had served as the city's largest employer, with a workforce of more than 20,000.

Painting of a TWA Constellation taking off from Municipal Airport, Kansas City, Missouri
Painting by Douglas Rowe
Source: The TWA Museum, The Charles B. Wheeler Downtown Airport, Kansas City, Missouri

TWA was destined to become one of the major players in air transportation, competing with American, United and Eastern airlines and later with Pan American. In 1930, Postmaster General Walter F. Brown called for the merger of Transcontinental Air Transport (TAT) with Western Air Express. The new carrier was formed on October 1, 1930, as Transcontinental & Western Air (T&WA). The merger was the result of the "Spoils Conference" and "Airmail Act," with Brown controlling the awarding of airmail contracts and routes.

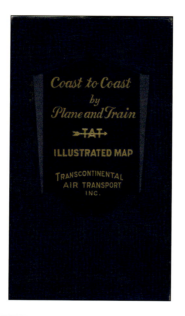

**Top row and bottom left: Record of the inaugural 1928 flight
launching 48-hour transcontinental service via plane and train**

**Right: The passenger list for the inaugural flight included Amelia Earhart (third from left)
and Charles Lindbergh (third from right)**

Source, all: The TWA Museum, Charles B. Wheeler Downtown Airport, Kansas City, Missouri

Multiple small aircraft companies were combined to form the enterprise that would become Trans World Airlines. Aero Corporation of California, organized in 1926, was one such company. Each of Aero's owners was an accomplished pilot: the group included Jack Frye, Paul Richter, and Walter Hamilton. Known as the "Three Musketeers of Aviation," they became important figures in the company's history.

Transcontinental brought the experience of famed aviator Charles Lindbergh to the merger. Western brought the business expertise of Jack Frye. In July of 1929, forty-eight-hour passenger service from coast to coast was inaugurated, combining the use of airplanes by day and railroads by night. With much fanfare and the draw of both Lindbergh and Amelia Earhart, the inaugural flight took off. By 1930, TWA was offering coast-to-coast flights exclusively by air, aboard one of the planes of the "Lindbergh Line," with a night's layover in Kansas City. TWA formally moved its administrative headquarters from New York to Kansas City in 1931.

Left: The first TWA hostess uniform worn by hostess Frances Ice in the early 1930s
Source: The TWA Museum, Charles B. Wheeler Downtown Airport, Kansas City, Missouri

Right: Early TWA promotional postcard
Source: The Tom Taylor Collection

A tragic incident that same year stands out among the company's early challenges. Flight 599 crashed near the town of Bazaar, Kansas. It was a public relations nightmare. Legendary Notre Dame football coach Knute Rockne was among the victims who died in the crash; he was headed to California to advise a film company. If there was a silver lining to the tragedy, it was the fact that the crash investigation brought about a radical change in aircraft design. Investigators concluded that the wood supporting the wings had failed. Jack Frye, vice-president of operations for TWA, soon pioneered the all-metal frame. Douglas Aircraft undertook construction of the new design, which was known as the DC-1.

Left: Postcard depicting an early TWA plane, bearing the inscription "The Lindbergh Line,"
at the Municipal Airport terminal, Kansas City, Missouri
Source: The Tom Taylor Collection
Right: Positioning of the TWA "Moonliner" atop the TWA administrative headquarters
Kansas City – 1956
Source: The Chris Wilborn Collection

In the mid-1930s, legal problems concerning the awarding of airmail contracts arose. TWA was declared ineligible to bid on such contracts, and the ownership of the company was restructured. The new airline group (TWA Inc.) saw Frye and Richter retaining partial ownership. They were joined by the Lehman Brothers Investment House and John D. Hertz, owner of Yellow Cab Company, who obtained controlling stock. At the end of 1934, Frye was promoted to president of the new company, and Richter became vice-president of operations. Walt Hamilton was named vice-president of mechanical operations. The airline began to experience real growth with the advent of new transports, DC-2s and Boeing "Stratoliners." The formation of the new fleet, with its pressurized cabins, resulted in higher-altitude routes and faster service. The growth was due in large part to the innovation of management, together with input from employees.

In 1939, Howard Hughes began purchasing shares in the company, and he eventually gained controlling interest. The entrepreneur bought a total of forty Lockheed Constellations. World War II became a boom time for TWA: the airline would fly more than forty million miles for the army during that conflict. After the war, and following the breakup of Pan American Airways' lock as the only recognized international carrier, TWA's worldwide routes skyrocketed. The previously cordial relationship between Frye and Hughes soon came to an end, with Hughes as the expected winner. Frye resigned in February of 1947, followed by Richter in April.

By the 1950s, changes were once again in store for TWA. The company's name was officially changed to Trans World Airlines, rather than Transcontinental & Western Air, Inc. The executive offices were moved from Kansas City to New York in the late 1950s, but the servicing of TWA's fleet of planes remained in Kansas City. The base was eventually moved from the Fairfax Airport in Kansas City, Kansas, to a massive overhaul base in Kansas City, Missouri. The 5,000-acre plot of land, first known as Mid-Continent International Airport (MCI), is now recognized as Kansas City International Airport (KCI). Also in the late 1950s, TWA became the first airline to hire an African American flight attendant, Margaret Grant.

The 1960s saw the relinquishing of power by Hughes, due to problems brought about by credit issues resulting from the airline's late entrance into the Jet Age. In 1961, Charles Tillinghast Jr. succeeded to the position of chairman of the board, continuing in that capacity until 1976. Various court actions against Hughes, including anti-trust verdicts, led to the divestiture of his holdings in 1966.

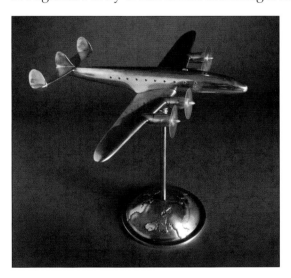

A model TWA Constellation provided by the company for display in the offices of travel agencies.
Source: The Nick Vedros Collection

Investor Carl Ichan purchased controlling interest in TWA in 1985. The honeymoon enjoyed by TWA and Kansas City was followed by a bitter divorce caused by irreconcilable differences. TWA filed for Chapter 11 bankruptcy in 1992. In 1993, after selling off most of TWA's profitable assets, Ichan was ousted. But it was too late: TWA again filed for bankruptcy in 1995. In 2001, the parent company of American Airlines acquired the enterprise. The mutually beneficial business relationship that had existed between Kansas City and TWA was over.

Nevertheless, traces of the love affair between TWA and Kansas City remain. Former employees, from mechanics to flight attendants and pilots, have rallied to keep the memories of the once-happy relationship alive. TWA memorabilia is highly collectible. The TWA Museum at the Kansas City Charles B. Wheeler Downtown Airport (formerly Municipal Airport) is staffed by an all-volunteer force. Housed in TWA's original headquarters at 10 Richards Road, the museum is well stocked with artifacts from throughout the airline's history. There you can view the well-preserved uniform worn by Frances Ice, an early flight attendant. You will see an original seat used aboard a 1929 Ford Tri-Motor plane and a large-scale model of a Boeing 747, along with thousands of photographs and collectibles. TWA was known for developing an overwhelming number of promotional items to attract passengers, and many are on display at the TWA Museum.

First Class food service items and early luggage tags
Source: The Tom Taylor Collection

Royal Ambassador first-class menu, plates, glasses, and coffee cup
Source: The Tom Taylor Collection

TWA's legacy includes many firsts in aviation history. It was the first airline to inaugurate around-the-clock and coast-to-coast passenger service, in addition to mail service. In collaboration with the Goodrich Rubber Company, it was the first airline to develop de-ice systems (1934). It was first to adopt the Sperry Automatic Pilot as standard equipment (1934); first to provide non-stop transcontinental service (1946); first to utilize a system on instantaneous flight reservations (1947); and first to serve freshly brewed coffee in flight (1957).

The Alpha Project

"There has never been a restoration in our experience that
can compare with the achievement by TWA's skilled volunteers."

—Robert K. Mikesh
The Smithsonian Institution

A display of airplanes suspended from the ceiling is usually among the first items to attract
your attention when you enter the main hall of the National Air & Space Museum in
Washington, DC. The planes offer an eye-popping look at the "Golden Age" of American
aviation. Charles Lindbergh's "Spirit of St. Louis" is perhaps the most recognizable artifact.
But included in the group is another flying machine worthy of study and admiration: a 1930
Northrop Alpha NC11Y used by TWA to deliver mail on transcontinental flights. It was a
romantic and highly dangerous era; only five such airplanes formed part of the short-lived
TWA fleet. Purchased by Frye, they were flown until their retirement in the mid-1930s.
The plane on display, designed by engineer Jack Northrop, stands as the sole survivor of that
fleet. Due to its innovations in aircraft development, it set the standard for air transport. The
Alpha NC11Y (or Northrop 4A, as it is otherwise known) was a single-engine plane that
revolutionized airframe design. It was Northrop's test of the concept of all-metal construction.

How the plane came to be rescued and restored is a shining example of the widely acclaimed
"Kansas City Spirit." In the words of Hallmark founder Joyce C. Hall, referring to
the town's unflagging courage and cooperative attitude following the Flood of 1951, it
demonstrated "what can be achieved when those with good hearts come together to accomplish
the impossible."

**The Northrop Alpha NC11Y airplane on display at the
National Air & Space Museum, Washington, DC**
*Source: The National Air & Space Museum, Washington, DC
Photo by Kathi and Michael Driggs*

 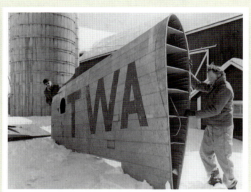

**The badly deteriorated Northrop Alpha transport plane
being rescued from a Wisconsin barn in mid-winter of 1975**
Source: The TWA Museum at the Charles B. Wheeler Downtown Airport, Kansas City, Missouri

After its retirement, the airplane passed through a series of owners. The Experimental Aircraft Association of Hales Corners, Wisconsin, was the last. The plane languished in a Wisconsin barn for years, suffering the indignities of time and deterioration. In 1974, representatives of the Smithsonian Institution set out to locate this lone survivor and have it restored in time for the nation's bicentennial and the opening of the new Air & Space Museum in 1976. Upon finding and rescuing the badly deteriorated body of the plane, the Smithsonian approached volunteers from TWA to undertake the task of bringing the plane back to life. 1976 was also the company's Golden Jubilee anniversary. A group of retired TWA employees graciously agreed to rebuild missing sections and restore the aircraft. The endeavor was led by Dan McGrogan, from its inception until the Alpha NC11Y was turned over to the Smithsonian in time for the Bicentennial celebration. McGrogan was a ground instructor in flight operations training at TWA's Jack Frye Training Center in Kansas City. The entire team took up the challenge to complete the work in eight short months. They dubbed their efforts the "Alpha Project" and adopted the motto: "The Spirit of '76."

The team's first challenge was to remove the pieces of the plane from the barn in Wisconsin and transport them back to TWA's overhaul base in Kansas City. There, in the shadows of 747s, 707s and other relics of the Jet Age, the workers began the painstaking work of restoring the plane to its original appearance and mechanical working condition. It was no easy task, requiring an overwhelming number of man hours, as well as mechanical skill and love on the part of the all-volunteer force. By all rights their efforts should have taken two years, but in the true "Kansas City Spirit" tradition, they achieved their goal in less than one.

From The Independence Examiner of January 26, 1976: "Project volunteers shrug off the claims of 'miracle.'" In the words of mechanic Carl Langston: "What it really represents is hard work, skill and devotion by about 50 mechanics, pilots, engineers, clerks and office people who cared enough to volunteer the time and energy to preserve an important piece of our heritage."

**The Northrop Alpha NC11Y at the TWA overhaul base in Kansas City,
being readied for its new home, The National Air and Space Museum**
*Source: The TWA Museum at the Charles B. Wheeler Downtown Airport,
Kansas City, Missouri*

**The restored Northrop Alpha at Kansas City International Airport
prior to delivery to the National Air and Space Museum
In this photo the Alpha is dwarfed by one of TWA's fleet of Lockheed L-1011s.**
Source: The TWA Museum, Charles B. Wheeler Downtown Airport, Kansas City, Missouri

The Hotel Baltimore Lobby
Source: Missouri Valley Special Collections, Kansas City Public Library

The Hotel Baltimore served as a luxurious and eclectic showcase
of the architect Louis Curtiss's craft, and he spared no extravagance.

– Bruce Mathews

THE HOTEL BALTIMORE

Hotel Baltimore, Kansas City, Mo.

Postcard view of Hotel Baltimore
Source: The Steve Noll Collection

When the 1900 Democratic National Convention opened in Kansas City, Missouri, the Hotel Baltimore hosted the party's nominee, William Jennings Bryan. At that time it was among the largest and most opulent hotels in the United States. For the next forty years it would continue to grow, both "physically and sentimentally," in the words of Kansas City architect Henry Van Brunt. But the Baltimore's lights dimmed all too soon.

Flamboyant Kansas City architect Louis Curtiss designed the masterpiece, which opened in 1899 at the southeastern corner of Eleventh Street and Baltimore Avenue. It boasted 160 large and well-appointed guest rooms. Between 1901 and 1908, the hotel underwent three major expansions, bringing the total number of rooms to 550. At that point it occupied the

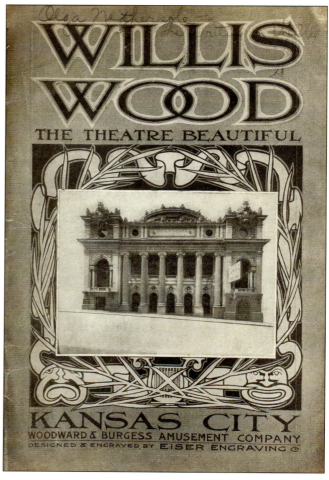

Willis Wood Theatre program cover and inside page advertising the Baltimore Hotel
Source, both: The Felicia Londré Collection

entire western half of the block, from Eleventh Street to Twelfth Street, and from Main Street to Baltimore Avenue.

The watchful eye of railroad magnate Bernard Corrigan was an ever-present fixture during the construction of the hotel, which stood on property owned by the Corrigan family. It was not the last project that Corrigan and Curtiss would work on together: in 1913, Curtiss designed a magnificent home for Corrigan at the northwestern corner of Fifty-fifth Street and Ward Parkway. The house is listed on the National Register of Historic Places.

Three years after the construction of the Baltimore Hotel, Col. Willis Wood chose Curtiss to design the 1,500-seat Willis Wood Theatre, which stood at a diagonal across Eleventh Street and which cost more than $400,000 to build. The proximity of the two properties led to a unique connection: an underground tunnel running from the hotel's Heidelberg Bar to the men's smoking room on the theatre's lower level. On performance nights the tunnel, dubbed "Highball Alley," was a busy place—particularly on evenings with inclement weather.

Top: Amelia Earhart in her room at the Baltimore Hotel, 1928
Below: Baltimore Hotel – Hoover Headquarters, 1928 Republican National Convention
Source, both: Missouri Valley Special Collections, Kansas City Public Library

The hotel served as a luxurious and eclectic showcase of Curtiss's craft, and the architect had spared no extravagance. Curtiss designed the hotel's exterior in Italian Renaissance style, while the interior featured Greek detailing and Roman Empire touches. Marble appeared throughout, and all ceilings were sculpted. The hotel's predominant color scheme was ivory with touches of pale and dark green. Guest rooms were airy and bright, with large windows that allowed the entry of light, even on the darkest

Hotel Baltimore china
Source: The Abigail and Fred Tempel Collection

Hotel Baltimore china
Sources: The Tom Taylor Collection

Hotel Baltimore china
Source: The Abigail and Fred Tempel Collection

Hotel Baltimore silver serving platter
Source: The Patricia Cleary Miller Collection

Hotel Baltimore china
Source: The Abigail and Fred Tempel Collection

days of winter. The guest registry could have doubled as an impressive listing of "Who's Who" in America. Featured on its pages were the names of Presidents William Howard Taft and Theodore Roosevelt; presidential hopeful William Jennings Bryan; boxing great John L. Sullivan; actress Ethel Barrymore; author Henry Miller; actor Richard Mansfield; and world-renowned aviator Amelia Earhart.

The lavish public areas included the Pompeiian and Renaissance rooms, which together could accommodate 800 dinner guests. A 730-square-foot dance floor and orchestral stage made an unforgettable impression.

Hotel Baltimore furniture
Source: The Patricia Cleary Miller Collection

Hotel Baltimore furniture
Source: The Patricia Cleary Miller Collection

Hotel Baltimore furniture
Source: The Patricia Cleary Miller Collection

Photo from Hotel Baltimore's Pompeiian Room, featuring a marble urn
Source: Missouri Valley Special Collections, Kansas City Public Library

The same urn now located in Mission Hills, Kansas

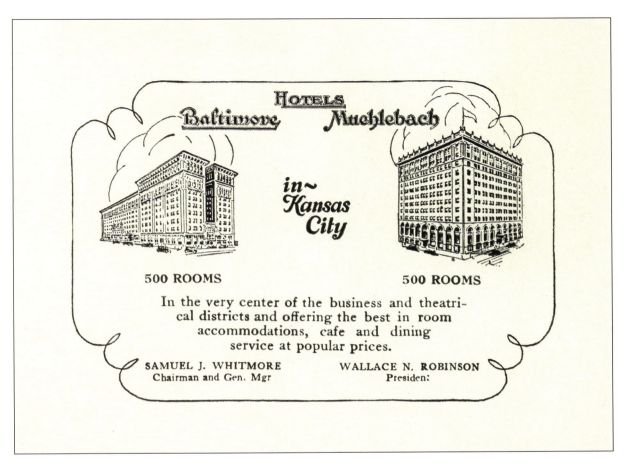

**Advertisement for Baltimore and Muehlebach Hotels
when both were under the management of Barney Allis**
Source: The Michael Bushnell Collection

An elegant marble urn once graced the Pompeiian Dining Room. When the hotel ceased operations in 1938, J. C. Nichols, developer of the famed Country Club Plaza district and other exclusive residential districts, purchased the beautiful vessel. It stands today as a silent sentinel on an island of its own, just north of Tomahawk Road on Wenonga Terrace in Mission Hills, Kansas.

Many reasons for the hotel's 1938 closure may be identified, including the fact that operating expenses were made even more untenable by the Great Depression. The Muehlebach Hotel had debuted during the Baltimore's era. The newer hostelry proved to be the winner of the tacit competition, despite the fact that the Baltimore had undergone an extensive (and expensive) renovation in 1914. In 1928, the two hotels merged; both were managed by Barney Allis. Four years later, Corrigan Realty took back the hotel and operated it for its final six years. By that time, the once-grand Willis Wood Theatre had been consumed by flames. Bernard Corrigan, the visionary who nurtured the hotel into existence and oversaw each of its expansions, had died. Like the light that had shined brightly through its windows for four decades, the Baltimore's life was also extinguished.

Muehlebach Hotel china
Source: The Tom Taylor Collection

THE HOTEL MUEHLEBACH

BALTIMORE AVENUE AND WYANDOTTE AVENUE AT TWELFTH STREET

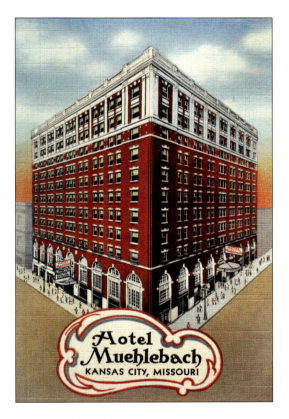

Muehlebach Hotel postcard
Source: The Steve Noll Collection

Fewer than twenty years after the opening of the Baltimore Hotel, a new kid on the block arrived in Kansas City. The hotel was the dream of entrepreneur George Muehlebach, who had made a fortune from a variety of businesses that included farming, saddlery, vineyard operation, and running a brewery bearing his name. Unfortunately, Muehlebach's death in 1905 prevented him from fulfilling his ambition. His son, George E. Muehlebach, would make the fantasy a reality. Construction began in 1913. The Muehlebach Hotel opened on May 17 of 1915, encompassing a substantial portion of the city block from Baltimore Avenue to Wyandotte Avenue and Twelfth Street to Thirteenth Street. The new hostelry opened with great fanfare as five hundred balloons were released from the rooftop. Missouri Governor Elliott Major was first to sign the guest register.

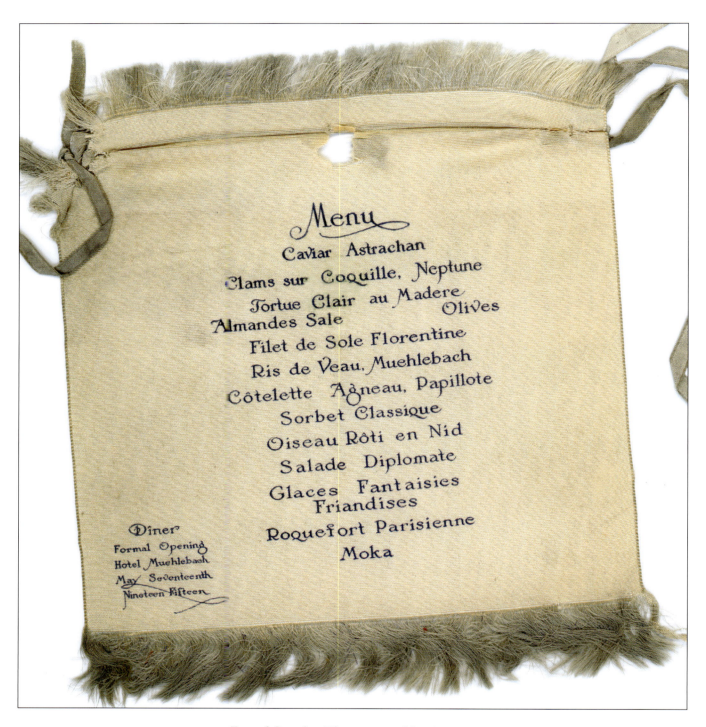

Formal Opening Dinner menu, May 17, 1915
Source: Missouri Valley Special Collections, Kansas City Public Library

China used at the Muehlebach Hotel after its 1915 opening
Source: Raphael Hotel Group

Later period china from the Hotel Muehlebach
Sources: left: The Philip and Nancy Reicher Collection; right: The Steve Noll Collection

The Muehlebach was proud to celebrate its one-hundredth anniversary in 2015. Numerous renovations and expansions have taken place during the hotel's first century, including several changes of ownership. Fortunately, a series of highly qualified managers have overseen and guided the Muehlebach through each stage of its development.

Left: Hotel Muehlebach room key *Source: The Steve Noll Collection*
Right: 1939 VIP Card signed by Barney Allis *Source: The Steve Noll Collection*

Café Picardy match holder
Source: The Steve Noll Collection

Terrace Grill ashtray
Source: Raphael Hotel Group

Hotel Muehlebach serving platter
Source: The Steve Noll Collection

Hotel Muehlebach footed bowls
Source: The Tom Taylor Collection

FOUNDING OF SPEBSQSA
MUEHLEBACH HOTEL - 1938
In the lobby of this Hotel
Owen C. Cash and Rupert I. Hall of Tulsa, Oklahoma
Met by chance in the year 1938.
Their meeting resulted in the formation of an impromptu
Barbershop Quartet which sang on these very premises.
This experience so enriched the lives of these men that
upon their return to Tulsa they formed the
Society for the Preservation and Encouragement of
Barber Shop Quartet Singing in America.
Today SPEBSQSA is the Largest all Male
Singing Fraternity in the World.
PRESENTED BY
BOARD OF DIRECTORS, SPEBSQSA, INC.
On the occasion of its Twenty-Fifth Anniversary, April 11, 1963

A chance meeting in the lobby of the Hotel Muehlebach in 1938 led
to the founding of the Society for the Preservation and Encouragement
of Barber Shop Quartet Singing in America (SPEBSQSA).

Nevertheless, much has remained the same throughout the decades. The renowned hostelry has built a lasting legacy of excellent service and attention to detail in every aspect. Known for its charm and comfort, the Hotel Muehlebach will also be remembered for its fine dining and notable guests. The list of luminaries found in the guest book reads like a virtual compendium of the world's political leaders, dignitaries, and celebrities. In 1916, President Theodore Roosevelt became the first of sixteen American presidents to stay at the Muehlebach. Others included Ford, Johnson, Kennedy, Reagan, Franklin Roosevelt, and, of course, Truman. During Kansas City's "Golden Age of Theatre," numerous performers from houses such as the Shubert, Willis Wood, Auditorium, Standard, Newman, and Orpheum chose the Muehlebach as their temporary home. The list of stars boasts Mae West, Eddie Foy, Gloria Swanson, Mary Pickford, Al Jolson, and "Big Band" leaders Tommy Dorsey, Benny Goodman, and Guy Lombardo. Additional well-known guests included baseball greats Joe DiMaggio, Babe Ruth, and Lou Gehrig. Military leaders in the registry include the five World War I generals who came to Kansas City for the 1921 site dedication of the Liberty Memorial. Dwight D. Eisenhower spent time at the Muehlebach upon his triumphant return to the United States at the end of World War II, as did Gen. Omar Bradley.

The hotel has been the backdrop of much of Kansas City's history. In 1922, the Coon Sanders Night Hawks became the first band to play a regular radio program, broadcasting over Station WDAF from the Muehlebach's Plantation Grill. In 1938, a chance meeting between two businessmen from Tulsa who were marooned in a snowstorm led to the formation of the Barber Shop Harmony Society. In 1948, the Belles of the American Royal, also known as BOTAR, was formed at the Muehlebach in support of the ongoing legacy of the American Royal and Kansas City's agricultural roots.

Jean Harlow

Mary Pickford

Eddie Foy

Ethel Barrymore

Gen. Omar Bradley

Al Jolson

Pres. Theodore Roosevelt

Pres. Harry S. Truman

Babe Ruth

A few of the guests of the Hotel Muehlebach
Sources: The Strauss-Peyton Collection at the Jackson County Historical Society,
The Dick Rees Collection and The Library of Congress, Washington, DC

OWNERS AND GENERAL MANAGERS

The hotel was first operated under a lease arrangement between the Muehlebach Estate and the Mid-Continent Hotel Company. Joseph Reichl was the first general manager of the new 500-room hostelry.

The Trianon Hotel Company, led by hotelier Barney Allis, bought the hotel in 1931. The purchase was made possible with a $130,000 loan from banker James Kemper. Allis was demanding, energetic, and sometimes dictatorial; his attention to detail and devotion to the comfort of his guests made him a legend in the hotel industry.

In 1954, Allis convinced Philip Pistilli, a recent graduate of the prestigious School of Hotel Administration at Cornell University, to come to Kansas City and work for him. A bond of friendship was formed that would last until Allis's passing. Having worked his way up under the tutelage of Allis, Pistilli was promoted to vice-president and general manager in 1962. Throughout his career, he would be known for the opportunities he afforded for women, as well as special needs workers.

Allis sold the hotel to New York financier Joseph Lubin in 1962. Three months after the sale, the entrepreneur collapsed and died on the street in front of the Aladdin Hotel, next door to the Muehlebach. Ironically, one of Allis's famous mottos was: "Never die in your own hotel." It was a rule he managed to obey, but it was a close call.

In 1974, the Equitable Life Insurance Company acquired the hotel, although it continued operations as the Radisson Muehlebach. In 1987 the hotel was purchased by the Morgan Group and was managed by the Raphael Hotel Group, which was led by Philip Pistilli. Pistilli had formed the Raphael Hotel Group, which wisely purchased the Vista International. Pistilli renamed the hotel the Allis Plaza, in honor of his lifelong mentor. Five years later, the hotel became a Marriott franchise, taking the name of the Marriott Kansas City Downtown.

In 1995 the then-empty Muehlebach and the Marriott Kansas City Downtown were purchased by the Kansas City Downtown Hotel Group. After constructing the new 410-room Muehlebach Tower and renovating the meeting, convention, and dining rooms, the Muehlebach merged with the Marriott Kansas City Downtown. With 983 rooms, the Kansas City Marriott Downtown became the largest hotel in Kansas City. The expansion included a walkway over Wyandotte Avenue and Twelfth Street that ingeniously connects the two buildings.

Following Philip Pistilli's death in 2003, his son Kevin ably assumed the leadership role of the Raphael Hotel Group. Kevin continues his father's legacy as president, and he handles the overall operations of the company's holdings. The leaf has not fallen far from the tree.

WHITE HOUSE WEST

Of the many presidents who have been guests at the hotel, the most frequent was President Harry S. Truman. He stayed at the Muehlebach so often that it became unofficially known as the "White House West." In 1947, during his first term in office, Truman signed the landmark Truman Doctrine in the hotel's Presidential Suite. The Truman Doctrine pledged political, military and economic assistance to all democratic nations under threat from external or internal authoritarian forces. The table was subsequently used on two other occasions, after it was taken to the Harry S. Truman Library in Independence, Missouri. On July 30, 1965, President Lyndon B. Johnson used it to sign the Medicare Act. After the signing he presented the Trumans with the first two Medicare cards. Several decades later, on July 8, 1997, Secretary of State Madeleine Albright used the table to officially recognize the Czech Republic, Hungary, and Poland as members of NATO. After a quiet night's rest at the Elms Hotel in Excelsior Springs, Missouri, in 1948, Truman ventured to the Muehlebach to greet the press after his upset victory over Thomas E. Dewey. The hotel served as the Kansas City headquarters of the "Man from Missouri" until his years in office ended in 1953. In 1960, Truman chose the Muehlebach as the site for a campaign luncheon for John F. Kennedy.

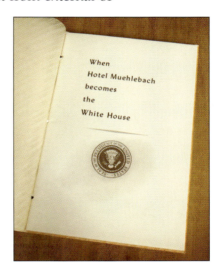

Brochure "When Hotel Muehlebach becomes the White House"
Source: The Harry S. Truman Library & Museum

The table used by President Truman to sign the document that became known as the Truman Doctrine
Source: The Harry S. Truman Library & Museum

The White House switchboard used at the Muehlebach Hotel when President Truman was a guest
Source: The Harry S. Truman Library & Museum

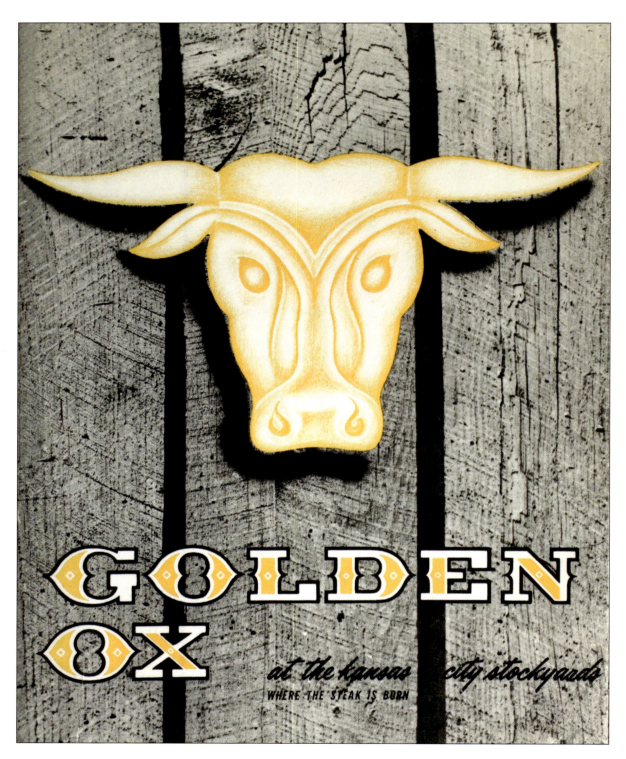

A menu cover from the Golden Ox restaurant
1600 Genessee Street, Kansas City, Missouri
Source: The Steve Noll Collection

THE GOLDEN OX

WHERE THE KANSAS CITY STRIP STEAK WAS BORN

**The iconic Golden Ox logo, menus and a
14-oz. bottle of Golden Ox steak sauce**
Source: The Steve Noll Collection

The Golden Ox restaurant opened for business in the Kansas City Livestock Exchange Building in May of 1949. For the following sixty-five years, it was a Midwestern dining institution. As anyone in the restaurant business will tell you, a run of that many years is almost unheard-of. But then, the Golden Ox, as we knew it, was no ordinary restaurant.

The legendary restaurant was founded by Jay B. Dillingham, who had begun work in the stockyards shortly after his 1935 marriage to Frances Thompson. Dillingham would serve as president of the Kansas City Stockyards Company from 1948 until 1975. His role as president included serving as landlord of the Golden Ox. The versatile entrepreneur was also president of the Kansas City Connecting Railroad Company, which was instrumental in coordinating the efforts of all other railroads that shipped cattle to the Kansas City stockyards.

American Royal steer, November 15, 1940
Source: The Chris Wilborn Collection

The restaurant was blessed by a built-in clientele from its inception. It owed its existence to the thousands of farmers and ranchers who brought their cattle, sheep, hogs, horses, and mules to the sprawling two-hundred-and-sixty-acre Kansas City Stockyards complex, the second-largest such operation in the country at that time. Other patrons included employees of the nearby packing houses, traders, and businessmen who conducted their affairs in the nine-story Livestock Exchange Building. It was there that the world-famous "Kansas City Strip Steak" was born.

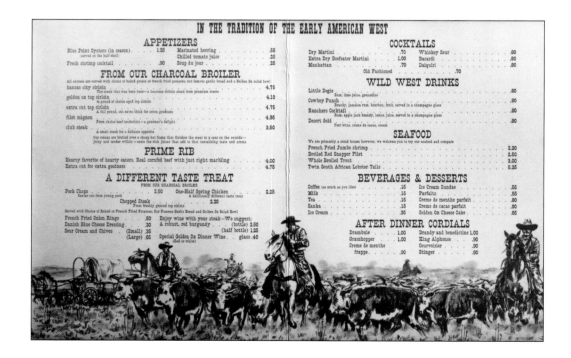

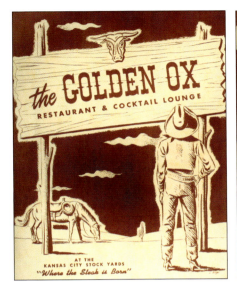

Selections from early Golden Ox menus
Source: The Steve Noll Collection

An early menu from the Golden Ox offered the Kansas City Sirloin for $3.90, an Extra-Cut Golden Ox Top Sirloin (three quarters of a pound of choice, aged top sirloin) for $3.00, a filet mignon for $4.25, and prime rib (extra cut for extra goodness) for $3.00. Additional fare appeared on the menu, but the Golden Ox was all about its steaks.

As the restaurant proudly boasted: "Our steaks are broiled under a sharp hot flame that finishes the meat to a sear on the outside – juicy and tender within – and seals the rich juices that add to that tantalizing taste and aroma."

One of the many wonderful Western Art treasures from the Golden Ox
Source: The Golden Ox restaurant

Although the Golden Ox enjoyed decades of serving the finest steaks, it was habitually beset by challenges. The first came in 1951, as a result of the infamous "Great Flood." That disaster devastated the stockyards, as well as the Livestock Exchange Building. Although Dillingham ordered the evacuation of the building, he himself had to be rescued. A motorboat made its way through the raging waters that had risen to thirty inches above the second floor. Dillingham had to lower himself into the boat by a rope suspended from a third-floor window. Since the Golden Ox was on the first floor of the building, we can only imagine the damage it suffered while underwater.

The Great Flood, July 15, 1951
Source: Missouri Valley Special Collections, Kansas City Public Library

The Golden Ox recovered from the 1951 flood and continued to serve choice steaks for more than sixty years afterward. In its heyday, as reported by Kansas City Star reporter Joyce Smith in 2003: "The Golden Ox was celebrated for its reasonably priced, top quality steaks that were aged on the premises, cut in the restaurant's own butcher shop and broiled over a charcoal flame. But it also gained fame for its cattle-baron décor of dark hardwoods, wagon-wheel chandeliers and burgundy carpet patterned with branding irons."

Golden Ox placemat
Source: The Steve Noll Collection

Golden Ox ashtray and swizzle sticks
Source: The Steve Noll Collection

Table candles from the Golden Ox
Left: "For Service Turn Shade"   Right: "Service Required"
Source: The Steve Noll Collection

Golden Ox stained-glass window created by Stew Langer
Source: The Golden Ox Restaurant

THE OWNERS

While Dillingham was preparing to open the Golden Ox, he enticed restaurateur Ralph Gaines to relocate from Chicago to Kansas City to manage the restaurant. Gaines ran the establishment until 1953, when, unbeknownst to Dillingham, he opened the Colony Steak House in direct competition with the Golden Ox. When Dillingham became aware of that disloyal act, he summoned Gaines into his office and demanded that he turn his keys over to the new manager, young Paul Robinson. Dillingham had recruited Robinson directly out of college in Oklahoma. Robinson, with co-founder Joe Gilbert, would go on to create the Gilbert/Robinson Company. That highly successful chain has restaurants throughout the country. Similarly, Dillingham did not confine the Golden Ox operations to Kansas City; other restaurants were opened in Denver (1958); in Washington, DC (1961); and Nashville (1968).

Left: Golden Ox credit card
Right: Golden Ox wine list and dinner coupons
Source: The Steve Noll Collection

Bill Rauschelbach began work at the Golden Ox in 1961. He was soon transferred to Washington, DC, where he would serve as the number-two man at that restaurant. Returning to Kansas City, he rose to the position of general manager by 1977. In 1990, Rauschelbach purchased the Golden Ox for $2.2 million. By 1997, Bill's son Jerry, along with his business partner Steve Greer, acquired ownership. Due to the collapsing economy, rising beef prices, and competition from strong national chains, the Rauschelbach ownership came to an end in 2003. Almost immediately, a group of investors led by Steve Greer and Bill Teel reopened "The Ox." Greer retired in 2014; but by that time, the "glory days" of the birthplace of the Kansas City Strip Steak had waned. The closing of Kemper Arena and the opening of the Sprint Arena played crucial roles in the demise of the Golden Ox. The relocation of the Future Farmers of America (FFA) from Kansas City also dealt a severe blow to the restaurant. The Golden Ox, as longtime patrons had known it, served its last dinner the night of December 20, 2014.

JAY B. DILLINGHAM
1910 – 2007

*He never strayed far from the old stock yards' way of doing business,
where 'a man's handshake' and 'a man's word' meant everything.*

—Daniel Coleman, Missouri Valley Special Collections, 2009

**John Dillingham with
his hat, American Royal – Past President belt buckle and cane**
Source: The John Dillingham Collection

The Kansas City Livestock Exchange Building, 1919
Source: The Chris Wilborn Collection

The 1951 flood signaled the beginning of the end for Kansas City's stockyards. Many of the packing houses in the area known as the West Bottoms closed. Ranchers began eliminating the stockyards as the "middleman," choosing to negotiate directly with other packers. The yards managed to survive for another forty years, finally closing on Halloween of 1991.

Jay Dillingham's son John relates a little-known fact about his father: "In the fall of 1949 the initial broadcast of WDAF-TV, owned by The Kansas City Star, was from the lobby of the Live Stock Exchange Building. It featured an interview of my father and Sen. Harry Darby by news anchor Randall Jesse." In 1951, as a follow-up feature, Randall Jesse and a cameraman braved the turbulent flood waters and returned to the site, reporting on the damage as they witnessed it.

Jay Dillingham's efforts after the 1951 flood are often described as heroic. The disaster occurred in July, and the annual American Royal Livestock Show was scheduled to open in October. Thanks to Dillingham's strong work ethic and leadership skills, along with the determination of thousands of citizens who pulled together, the show went on. The nearly impossible was accomplished with true "Kansas City Spirit." Jay Dillingham possessed that spirit in spades.

While Dillingham's role in the growth of the stockyards in Kansas City was vital, his lasting impact upon the entire region should not be overlooked. He possessed an innate ability to build relationships and bridge divides. He was a "Northlander" at heart. His and his wife's families settled in Clay and Platte counties, where they left a proud and lasting legacy. There has always been a lack of understanding of each other's needs north and south of the Missouri River on the Missouri side of the state line. This can also be said of the bi-state rivalries east and west of the state line dating back to the days leading up to the Civil War. Jay Dillingham worked seven days a week his entire life, not only on behalf of the cattle industry, but for all Kansas Citians, north, south, east and west.

Jay Dillingham was the only person to serve as president of both the Greater Kansas City Chamber of Commerce and the Kansas City, Kansas, Chamber of Commerce. He was appointed chairman of the Missouri Highway Commission by both Democratic and Republican governors. He maintained close relationships with presidents Truman and Eisenhower. He promoted Kansas City's annexation of land in the area known as the Northland. Dillingham campaigned for major flood control projects after witnessing the devastating effects of the 1951 flood. Missouri Governor John Dalton appointed him to the Missouri Public Water Resources Board; the improvements made by that body played a crucial role in reducing the damaging effects from the 1993 flood. Dillingham was vitally instrumental in relocating the city's main airport from the landlocked downtown Municipal Airport to the sprawling grounds of the Mid-Continent Airport in the Northland, which was proudly renamed Kansas City International Airport. Without his efforts, the metropolitan area's interstate highway system would surely have lagged behind. A Kansas City Star editorial dubbed him as "The Father of I-435," an expressway serving as a vital link for area motorists. Dillingham was a most worthy recipient of the title "Mr. Kansas Citian," an honor bestowed upon him by the Greater Kansas City Chamber of Commerce.

McDonald's Happy Meal
10th Anniversary
1977 – 1987

To Robert A. Bernstein
Bernstein-Rein Advertising
Thank you for bringing the Happy Meal, a bold idea
to the McDonald's System.
Your insight and conviction truly has made McDonald's a
fun place for children for the past ten years!
McDonald's Corporation
September 1987

The original Happy Meal boxes and the award
given to creator Bob Bernstein from the McDonald's Corporation
Source: Bernstein-Rein Advertising

THE HAPPY MEAL

BORN IN KANSAS CITY

Kansas Citians born after the turn of the millennium are often unaware of the fact that the McDonald's Happy Meal has its roots right here in KC. The cleverly designed box of popular treats has been a marketing icon since its 1977 launching. It was such an innovative phenomenon that it set the standard for a new era of consumer advertising, and it has received the highest of compliments by being copied ever since its debut.

The Happy Meal was the brainchild of Bob Bernstein, president and CEO of Bernstein-Rein Advertising. It will always be an outstanding part of his legacy—the "fun part."

In Bob's words: "The design of the Happy Meal box came from watching my oldest son Steve eat his breakfast while reading cereal boxes. When asked why he would read the boxes over and over again, he shrugged and said it was just something to do while he ate. The inspiration for creating the Happy Meal was born.

"The concept came at a time when McDonald's was in need of a children's meal. Moms were tired of splitting sandwiches, drinks and fries among the children. The kids needed their own meal. What made the Happy Meal special was the design of the container, which was a uniquely designed box with a handle. On the outside there were at least ten different games and puzzles to play or read while they ate. Inside every box was a child's surprise gift. What a Happy Meal!

"The Happy Meal was actually the last of a series of promotions I had developed for McDonald's over the preceding ten years, including: the Flying Hamburger, a Styrofoam airplane in the shape of a McDonald's hamburger; the Happy Cup, a yellow plastic cup with Ronald McDonald chasing his flying hamburger printed around the outside of the cup; Pencil Puppets, erasers that fit on the end of pencils in the shape of McDonald-land characters; Happy Lids, which snap on soft drinks in the shape of Frisbees; and the Sippy Dipper Straw, a plastic straw for kids in the shape of the Golden Arches."

While it was his concept, Bernstein is quick to acknowledge that it was the talented Kansas City-based art directors and marketing people at Bernstein-Rein who helped make the Happy Meal possible.

To forever perpetuate the courage, loyalty and sacrifice of the patriots
Who offered and who gave their services,
Their lives and their all,
In defense of liberty and the nation's honor during the World War

Medallion worn at the Liberty Memorial Dedication, November 1, 1921
Source: The Karol O'Brien Collection

To help defray costs for hosting the 1921 site dedication, the Liberty Memorial Association authorized production of eleven thousand medallions. They were sold for one dollar each. As a result, the sale not only covered all of the expenses for the event, it also enabled the group to realize a profit of seven thousand dollars.

THE LIBERTY MEMORIAL

DEDICATIONS, REDEDICATIONS, AND OFFICIAL CEREMONIES

On November 11, 1918, the Armistice was signed. It was intended to bring about an end to the so-called Great War, which was also known as "The War to End All Wars." For the next three years, in true "Kansas City Spirit" fashion, funds were raised, plans were drawn, and preparations were made to construct a lasting memorial to the men and women who had sacrificed so much. The new structure would stand on a lofty hill, just south of Kansas City's Union Station. The image of that important terminal had been forever etched on the memories of thousands of soldiers who passed through Kansas City on their way to or from the horrific conflict.

Shortly after the war, at the request of Mayor James Cowgill and the City Council, a group of forty Kansas City business and civic leaders stepped forward to form the Liberty Memorial Association, the goal of which was to raise funds to turn the vision of a memorial into a reality. In less than a year, they raised more than $2.5 million. The group was also charged with

The Liberty Memorial – December 5, 2006

guiding the project through completion. Lumber baron R. A. Long was selected as the organization's president, and developer J.C. Nichols served as vice-president. Other members included attorney Frank Sebree; bankers James M. Kemper and Rufus Crosby Kemper; philanthropist and businessman William Volker; and landscape architect George Kessler. Volker helped to acquire the land upon which the memorial was built, while Kessler designed the site's landscape plan. (Note: Kessler died in 1923, prior to the project's completion.)

After a lengthy competition to select an appropriate design, the association chose the "Flame of Inspiration" motif created by New York architect H. Van Buren Magonigle. A century later, merely standing in the commanding presence of the Jarvis Hunt-designed Union Station and the Magonigle-designed World War I Memorial remains an emotional experience.

GROUNDBREAKING AND SITE DEDICATION
November 1, 1921

A remarkable photograph taken the morning of November 1, 1921, features Jacob and Ella Loose as they stand on the patio of their mansion on fashionable Armour Boulevard, together with Gen. Armando Diaz of Italy and his military entourage. One might wonder what had brought an Italian general to Kansas City, and why he was photographed with the Looses. In fact, Diaz was in town to attend the momentous dedication of the Liberty Memorial. The couple had invited him to their stately home on the morning of the ceremony.

Jacob and Ella Loose with Gen. Armando Diaz of Italy on the side porch of their mansion prior to the dedication of the Liberty Memorial site, November 1, 1921
Source: The Chris Wilborn Collection

The five attending generals as featured in the Daniel MacMorris mural at the Liberty Memorial
Source: The National World War I Museum

Gen. Marshal Ferdinand Foch of France, Supreme Commander of the Allied Forces during World War I; Gen. John J. Pershing, Commander of the American Expeditionary Forces in France; Adm. Lord Beatty of Great Britain; and Lt. Gen. Baron Jacques of Belgium also participated in the dedication. On that day in Kansas City, Missouri, these five generals, each of whom played a pivotal role in the Great War, met together for the first time.

The generals and their hosts joined Vice-President Calvin Coolidge, sixteen governors, a multitude of other dignitaries, and more than 100,000 patriotic citizens to take part in Liberty Memorial's groundbreaking and site dedication. It had been scheduled during the third annual meeting of the American Legion, also held in Kansas City.

The saga of the memorial's construction was but another defining chapter in the story of the "Kansas City Spirit." Some thirty years later, after the Flood of 1951, Hallmark founder Joyce C. Hall defined said spirit as "that something special in the human heart that enables us to come together to accomplish the impossible."

And so it was in Kansas City, following the Armistice signifying the end of the Great War.

1921 American Legion parade at 18th and Grand as it passed the Kansas City Star building
Source: The Chris Wilborn Collection

**Official program of the Third National Convention
of the American Legion
Held concurrently in Kansas City with the 1921 site
dedication of the Liberty Memorial**
Source: The National World War I Museum

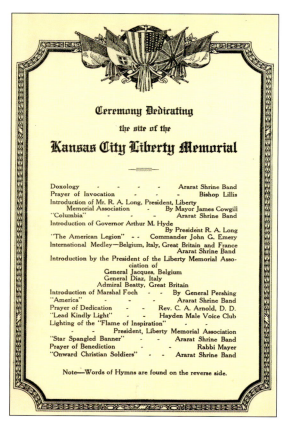

**November 1, 1921, Liberty Memorial site
dedication program**
Source: The National World War I Museum

**Italy's General Armando Diaz salutes the throngs gathered for the
1921 dedication of the Liberty Memorial**
Source: The National World War I Museum

**Britain's Admiral David Beatty (left) and Liberty Memorial Association President
Robert A. Long (center) depart from the Long Mansion, Corinthian Hall,
for the 1921 site dedication ceremonies**
Source: National World War I Museum

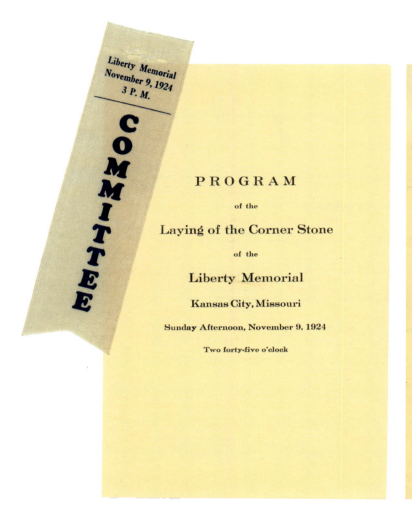

**Program of the Laying of the Cornerstone
of the Liberty Memorial, November 9, 1924**
Source: Missouri Valley Special Collections, Kansas City Public Library

On Sunday afternoon, November 9, 1924, local officials, members of the Liberty Memorial Association, and the citizens of Kansas City once again convened at the site of the Liberty Memorial. This time they gathered for the laying of the cornerstone of the magnificent tower. The festivities included a band concert and an airplane flyover under the command of Lt. Isaiah Davis. A cannon salute was followed by the Boy Scout Bugle Corps sounding the "Call to Worship."

The invocation was delivered by Rev. Elton Harris. Mayor Albert Beach introduced R. A. Long, president of the Liberty Memorial Association, who restated the purpose of the memorial as he addressed the crowd. Brig. Gen. Harry A. Smith appeared next on the agenda. Frank Sebree and J.C. Nichols, vice-presidents of the association, concluded by reading messages from President Calvin Coolidge, as well as each of the four generals and Adm. Beatty.

Among the items enclosed in the cornerstone were a record of the deceased soldiers of Kansas City and Jackson County; the President's Declaration of War; the Armistice Agreement of November 11, 1918; messages from Coolidge, Beatty, Foch, Jacques, Diaz, Pershing and Long; a film featuring four hundred feet of motion pictures of returning troops; news clips from the war and the site dedication of November 1, 1921; the Constitution of the United States; and the Bible.

The items placed in the Liberty Memorial during the 1924 Cornerstone laying
Source: The National World War I Museum

Laying of the Liberty Memorial Cornerstone 1924
Source: The National World War I Museum

MEMORIAL DEDICATION
November 11, 1926

Five years after the site dedication of the Liberty Memorial, President Coolidge once again returned to Kansas City. He came to dedicate the nearly completed memorial itself. In his dedicatory remarks, the President noted: "Today I return in order that I may place the official sanction of the National Government upon one of the most elaborate and impressive memorials that adorn our country." The following is an excerpt from his speech:

"It is with a mingling of sentiments that we come to dedicate this memorial. Erected in memory of those who defended their homes and their freedom in the World War, it stands for service and all that service implies. Reverence for our dead, respect for the living, loyalty to the country, devotion to humanity, consecration to religion, all of these and much more is represented in this towering monument. It has not been raised to commemorate war and victory, but rather the results of war and victory, which are embodied in peace and liberty. In its impressive symbolism it pictures the story of that one increasing purpose declared by the poet to mark all the forces of the past which finally converge in the Spirit of America in order that our country as 'the heir of all the ages, in the foremost of time,' may forever hold aloft the glowing hope of progress and peace to all humanity."

Coolidge was joined by Queen Marie of Romania, a daughter of Queen Victoria. Queen Marie was distinguished in her own right, through her writings and service with the Red Cross during the War.

On that occasion the crowd was more than half-again the size of that present at the site dedication of 1921. More than 150,000 citizens bore witness to the event. The mood was quite different from that of the earlier event: while the presence of the five generals in 1921 had set an international tone, the crowd of 1926 exuded an air of national pride.

Crowd gathered for the 1926 dedication of the Liberty Memorial
Source: The National World War I Museum

**President Calvin Coolidge speaking at the 1926
Liberty Memorial dedication**
Source: The Chris Wilborn Collection

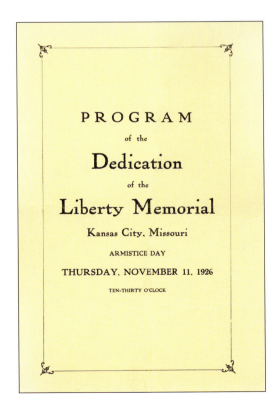

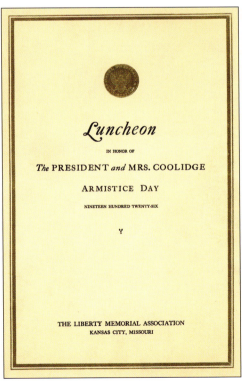

Liberty Memorial dedication and luncheon programs, November 11, 1926
Source, both: The National World War I Museum

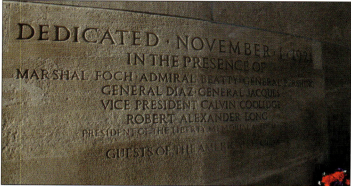

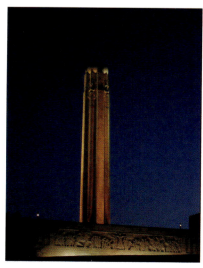

Tributes inscribed at the Liberty Memorial

DEDICATION OF THE GREAT FRIEZE
November 6, 1935

The Liberty Memorial tower and Great Frieze

"These have dared bear the torches of sacrifice and service.
Their bodies return to dust but their works liveth evermore.
Let us strive to do all which may achieve and cherish
a just and lasting peace among ourselves and with all nations."

—Inscription on the North Frieze

The Great Frieze was dedicated nine years after the tower itself was created by American sculptor and educator Edmund Amateis, under the direction of the Wight & Wight architectural firm. It is carved into the immense north wall, below the tower and memorial halls. The frieze, epic in its scale and content, depicts sequences of the Great War and a celebration of peace. The Great Frieze measures 19 feet in height by 145 feet in length.

REDEDICATION
November 11, 1961

THE LIBERTY MEMORIAL REDEDICATION
To the cause of understanding and friendship
amongst all the world's people

The Liberty Memorial was originally dedicated "to the patriots who gave their lives and services in World War I." The intent of the 1961 ceremony was to rededicate the memorial "to the people of the world as a symbol of understanding." The rededication was spearheaded by a group of local business and civic leaders. Chairman Joyce C. Hall expressed the sentiments the group hoped to achieve in building "a rallying point for the peoples of the world who could work together to achieve the understanding so urgently needed in the world today."

On November 10, 1961, at 11:00 a.m., the multitudes once again gathered at the base of the Liberty Memorial. It was Veterans Day. Former Presidents Eisenhower and Truman were on the agenda, as were Missouri Governor J.M. Dalton and Kansas Governor John Anderson Jr. Mayor H. Roe Bartle introduced Hall, and the rededication scroll was unveiled. After his introduction by Hall, Eisenhower spoke about the "People-to-People" program he had instituted in 1956. The following day, November 11, 1961, Truman delivered a stirring keynote address.

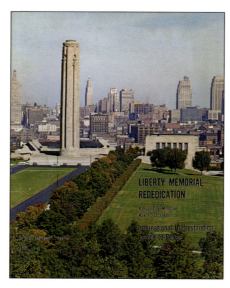 

Left: Liberty Memorial Rededication program, November 11, 1961
Right: Former President Harry S. Truman speaking at the Rededication
Source, left: The Chris Smart Collection
Source, right: The Harry S. Truman Library & Museum

Joyce C. Hall, Chairman
The 1961 Liberty Memorial Rededication Committee
Source: The National World War I Museum

MEMORIAL CLOSES
November 9, 1994

Due to years of neglect and deferred maintenance, the memorial was declared unsafe for public use. The museum closed on November 9, 1994, remaining in that state until funding could be secured for restoration.

SALES TAX MEASURE PASSED TO RESTORE THE MEMORIAL
August 4, 1998

Once again, the "Kansas City Spirit" came to the fore. On August 4, 1998, voters in Kansas City authorized an eighteen-month, half-cent sales tax to restore the existing memorial and to fund the building of a new museum to display archives that had been presented to the memorial since the end of the Great War in 1918. Contributions from the citizens of Kansas City, the State of Missouri and the federal government, together with private donations, allowed the restoration to move forward.

Fundraising poster
Source: The Anita Gorman Collection

LISTING ON THE NATIONAL REGISTER OF HISTORIC PLACES
October 6, 2000

The formal application for inclusion of the Liberty Memorial on the National Register of Historic Places (NRHP) was prepared by Cydney E. Millstein, architectural historian. It was dated April 3, 2000. The massive document was submitted on behalf of the Kansas City, Missouri, Parks and Recreation Department. For those desiring more information about the history of the memorial than this volume will allow, the application, which can be found online, is a must-read. It was approved on October 6, 2000.

REDEDICATION
May 25, 2002

Following the successful campaign to raise funds, the Liberty Memorial was rehabilitated between 2000 and 2002. It was rededicated once again on May 25, 2002.

Souvenirs from the 2002 Rededication of the Liberty Memorial
Source: The Anita Gorman Collection

THE NATION'S OFFICIAL WORLD WAR I MUSEUM
2004

In 2004, by an act of Congress, the Liberty Memorial was designated as the nation's official World War I Museum. It was a well-deserved designation for a museum not located on the National Mall in Washington, DC. The measure was signed into law by President George W. Bush as part of the 2005 Defense Authorization Bill.

Also in 2004, construction commenced on the 80,000-square-foot expansion of the Museum and Research Center, located below the Memorial Tower.

DESIGNATION AS A NATIONAL HISTORIC LANDMARK
September 20, 2006

In September of 2006, Secretary of the Interior Dirk Kempthorne officially declared the Liberty Memorial as a National Historic Landmark. Under the supervision of the National Park Service, significant historic sites can be so cited if they are determined to "possess exceptional value or quality in illustrating or interpreting the heritage of the United States."

OPENING AND DEDICATION
OF THE NATIONAL WORLD WAR I MUSEAM
December 2, 2006

On December 2, 2006, the National World War I Museum opened to the public. It became an instant success among tourists, researchers, student groups, and historians. Frank Buckles, the country's last surviving World War I veteran, visited the museum on Memorial Day of 2008. He was 108 at the time. Buckles, who passed away in 2011, is buried in Arlington National Cemetery.

Souvenirs from the 2006 Opening of the National World War I Museum
Source: The Anita Gorman Collection

RECOGNITION AS THE NATIONAL WORLD WAR I MEMORIAL
December 19, 2014

On December 11, 2014, Congress passed legislation designating the Liberty Memorial as the nation's official World War I memorial. On December 19, 2014, President Obama signed the legislation officially recognizing the site as the National WWI Museum and Memorial.

The previous Congressional action had designated the site as the National World War I Museum, but the action had not cited the Liberty Memorial as the nation's official World War I Memorial. This closing of the gap may seem slight, but such was not the case. The 2014 legislation recognized the memorial in similar fashion as the World War II Memorial on the National Mall. At the time, measures were underway to build a new World War I Memorial in Washington, DC, with the intention of naming it as the "official" memorial.

The campaign to convince Congress to designate Kansas City's Liberty Memorial as the official National WWI Museum and Memorial was not a simple one. But in the words of Dr. Matthew Naylor, president and CEO of the WWI Museum and Memorial: "We are grateful to each of the members of Congress, including Senators Claire McCaskill and Roy Blunt and Representatives Emanuel Cleaver, Sam Graves, and Kevin Yoder, for leading this effort to officially recognize the Liberty Memorial."

The circle is complete.

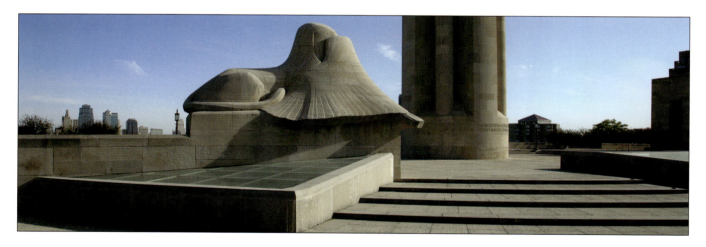

View of the south base of the tower, sphinx, deck and portion of the glass roof of the museum

A FEW OF THE MANY KANSAS CITIANS WHO SERVED DURING WORLD WAR I

Left to right: Capt. Carroll Barse Haff; Mrs. J. C. Nichols, Red Cross;
Dr. Clarence McGuire; James K. B. Hockaday

Left to right: Capt. Rufus Montgall; Lt. Walter H. Meyer;
Irwin Combs; Dr. H. Lewis Hess

*Sources: The Strauss-Peyton Collection at the Jackson County Historical Society,
the Library of Congress, the National World War I Museum and Memorial*

Stadium seats from Municipal Stadium, 1976
Source: The Mathews Family Collection

**O.K. Mathews and son Charlie, attending a Blues game
at Ruppert Stadium, 1939
(Starting in 1955 Ruppert Stadium became the site of Municipal Stadium)**
Source: The Mathews Family Collection

In a poignant connection for the author, I include two photographs that will always hold a special place in my heart. One of them features two seats from Municipal Stadium that were rescued the day before the stadium's demolition in 1976. The other captures my father, O.K. Mathews, and my oldest brother, Charlie, as they watched the Blues play during the 1939 season.

MUNICIPAL STADIUM

TWENTY-SECOND STREET AND BROOKLYN AVENUE – 1923 TO 1976

The Beatles, Harvey the Rabbit, Lamb Chop, the Wolf Pack, elephants, goats, mules, sheep…

No, they are not residents of a local animal farm. These characters once played leading roles in the history of Kansas City's original Municipal Stadium. They are reminders, treasured memories of professional sports played and concerts held in Kansas City's old Municipal Stadium. Built in 1923, the building stood at the northwestern corner of Twenty-second Street and Brooklyn Avenue. George E. Muehlebach, owner of the Kansas City Blues, the town's Minor League Baseball team, as well as the Muehlebach Beer Company and the Muehlebach Hotel, built the ballpark. Not unexpectedly, he named it Muehlebach Field.

Aerial view of Municipal Stadium
Twenty-second Street and Brooklyn Avenue, Kansas City, Missouri
Source: The Chris Wilborn Collection

THE BLUES

**Four members of the Kansas City Blues
were selected for the 1934 American Association All-Star Team**
Source: The Chris Wilborn Collection

The Kansas City Blues, members of the American Association, played their baseball games at Muehlebach Field from 1923 until the team was purchased in 1937. Col. Jacob Ruppert, owner of the New York Yankees, became the new owner. The Blues continued to play their home games at the field, but in the aptly renamed Ruppert Stadium. When the colonel passed away two years later, the site became known as Blues Stadium. The Minor League Blues Team, which was a farm club for the New York Yankees, continued to play in the stadium until 1954. Future stars like Bill "Moose" Skowron and Mickey Mantle saw their first game action with the Blues.

Following up on a 1927 exhibition game in Kansas City, Lou Gehrig came back for an exhibition game pitting the Yankees against the Blues on June 12, 1939. Sadly, this game became the last one that Gehrig would play in a Yankees uniform. The next day he boarded a train for the Mayo Clinic, where he learned he was suffering from amyotrophic lateral sclerosis (ALS). When he returned to New York, his playing days were over. Kansas City sports legends Tom Watson and George Brett have committed themselves to finding a cure for ALS, commonly known as "Lou Gehrig's Disease."

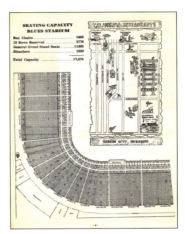

The 1946 Kansas City Blues official score book
Source: The Dave Starbuck Collection

Left: The KC Blues 1939 team photo Right: Mickey Mantle in his one year with the Blues
Source, both: The Dave Starbuck Collection

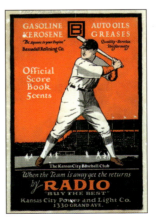

From the Kansas City Blues 1927 official score book
Source: The Dave Starbuck Collection

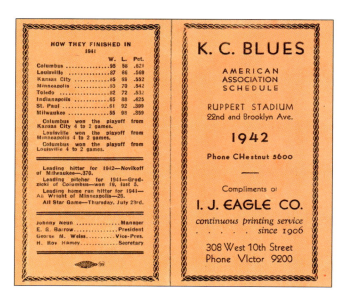

The Kansas City Blues 1942 schedule
Source: Missouri Valley Special Collections, Kansas City Public Library

The Kansas City Blues 1940 pitching staff
Source: The Chris Wilborn Collection

THE MONARCHS

The Kansas City Monarchs, members of the Negro Leagues, played their home games in Muehlebach Field between 1923 and 1931, and later from 1937 to 1954. The first Negro Leagues World Series was played at Muehlebach Field in 1924. The Monarchs fielded such greats as Satchel Paige, Buck O'Neil, James Thomas "Cool Papa" Bell, and Charles William "Bullet Joe"

Rogan, as well as legends Ernie Banks and Jackie Robinson. Robinson was on the Monarchs roster in 1945, when he was recruited by Walter O'Malley, owner of the Brooklyn Dodgers. He was the first African American to play in the Major Leagues. Ironically, that historic event contributed to the demise of the Negro Leagues: as an increasing number of African American players were signed by Major League teams, African American fans followed them. As a result, the Negro Leagues' fan base shrank to the point that the league was no longer sustainable.

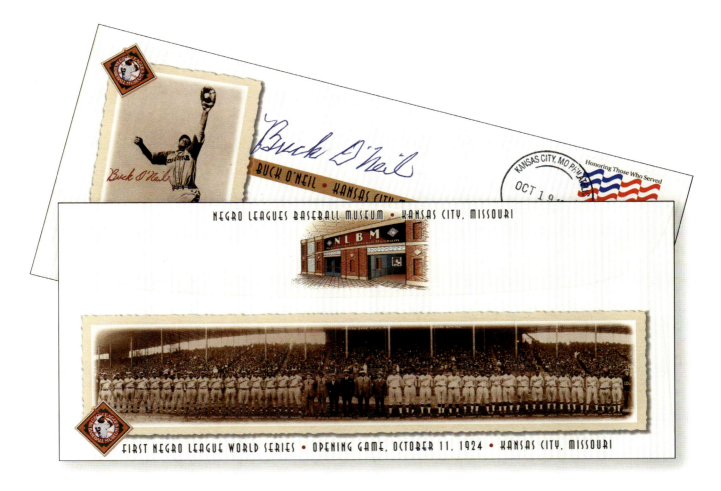

**A 1999 envelope created to recognize the Negro Leagues Baseball Museum,
the Kansas City Monarchs and opening day of the First Negro League World Series,
Kansas City, Missouri, October 11, 1924**
Source: Tension Envelope Corporation archives

Babe Ruth and Lou Gehrig visited Kansas City in 1927 as members of the New York Yankees. While in town, they presented an "ice box" to Dr. Katharine Berry Richardson at Children's Mercy Hospital, then located on Independence Boulevard. They stopped at the photography studio of Strauss-Peyton to have their pictures made, prior to playing in an exhibition game against the Monarchs. Their team consisted of other Major League all-stars. The Babe went 4 for 4, but to no avail. The All-Stars lost to the Monarchs.

JOHN J. "BUCK" O'NEIL

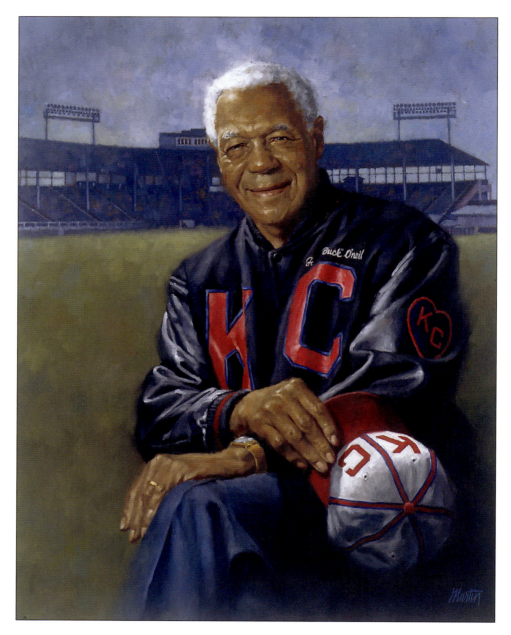

"Buck" O'Neil **by John Martin**

In 2012, when we completed *The Kansas City Spirit: Stories of Service Above Self*, I looked back upon the people we wrote about, those who had made Kansas City a better place in which to live. I thought about a couple of the characters who were "larger than life." One of them, Mayor H. Roe Bartle, was six feet, three inches tall, with a weight of more than 300 pounds. I also reflected upon Tony DiPardo, another heroic figure, who stood only five feet tall and weighed about 100 pounds. Both gentlemen contributed immensely to our quality of life.

Then I thought about John Jordan "Buck" O'Neil. Wasn't he larger than life? I decided that in my opinion, O'Neil demonstrated how life itself should be lived. His many accomplishments included being a player and manager in the Negro Leagues, as well as the first black coach in the Major Leagues. He was also a longtime scout for the Kansas City Royals. Even though he never made it into the Major League Baseball Hall of Fame, he was instrumental in helping scores of other Negro League players achieve that honor. Of course, O'Neil has a statue at the Hall in Cooperstown, in addition to an award presented in his name every three years. After his death in 2006, he was posthumously awarded the nation's highest civilian honor, the Presidential Medal of Freedom. But these accomplishments and recognitions are only a part of O'Neil's legacy.

The real story is that Buck O'Neil was one of those uniquely selfless individuals you meet along life's path. While many of his contemporaries were adversely affected by the hatred and discrimination they faced, the baseball legend never let such narrow-mindedness define who he was. He rose above it, writing that he was born "Right on Time." And at the Greater Kansas City Chamber of Commerce dinner following his death, when he received the "Kansas Citian of the Year" award (along with golfing great Tom Watson), he made a posthumous appearance on-screen, singing "The Greatest Thing in All of My Life is Loving You."

Buck O'Neil at the site of Municipal Stadium years after its demolition
Source: The Chris Wilborn Collection

THE ATHLETICS

In 1955, Kansas City moved up to the Major Leagues. The Kansas City Athletics took the field on a cold, snowy day in April. Their arrival in Kansas City was brought about by a chain of events starting with the 1953 purchase of the New York Yankees and Kansas City's Blues Stadium by Chicago real estate tycoon Arnold Johnson. The following year he purchased the Philadelphia A's from Connie Mack, with the intention of moving the A's to Kansas City. In doing so, Johnson sold the stadium to the city. In turn, Kansas City rented the ballpark back to Johnson until 1960, the year of his death.

Left: The first Major League Opening Day at Municipal Stadium, April 12, 1955
Source: Missouri Valley Special Collections, Kansas City Public Library
Right: The glove and ball used by Harry S. Truman
to throw out the first pitch, April 12, 1955
Source: The Harry S. Truman Library & Museum

The Minor League stadium built in 1923 seated a capacity crowd of approximately 17,000, which was not large enough for a Major League franchise in 1955. The old, one-level stadium was demolished, replaced by a new stadium with an upper deck and an increased seating capacity of about 30,000. Five thousand additional seats were added in 1961. Demolition of the original stadium was necessary after engineers determined that its piers would not support the weight of an upper deck.

Here's where the animals come in.

In 1960, Charlie Finley, a gentleman sometimes known as "The Grand Tinkerer," purchased the Kansas City A's. Constantly fiddling with the distances from home plate to the outfield walls was not enough for Finley. The new owner constructed a small zoo, complete with sheep and goats, behind the right field wall. His motive in purchasing the animals was to eliminate the need for hazardous mowing on the steep incline up to Brooklyn Avenue. The sheep and goats, however, were put in the perilous position of dodging home run balls to earn their keep.

The A's mascot was changed from an elephant to a mule, known in the annals of baseball lore as Charlie-O. (No comparisons between Charlie-O, the mule, and Charlie O., the owner, are needed here.) Carrying the animal theme one step further, Charlie O. (the owner) found it necessary to install a mechanical rabbit named Harvey behind home plate. Harvey the Rabbit assumed the role of rising out of the ground to turn over a new supply of baseballs to the home plate umpire whenever the need arose. At the same time, a contraption nicknamed "Little Blowhard" emerged from below ground to exhale compressed air over the dirty home plate. This maneuver supposedly allowed the home plate umpire to concentrate on the more urgent tasks at hand.

Left: Charlie-O, the Mule, with pitcher Ralph Terry and sons
Right: Charles O. Finley, A's owner, with Charlie-O, the Mule
Source: The Dave Starbuck Collection

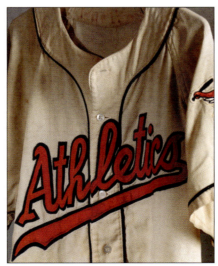

1956 A's uniform of player Mike Baxes
Source: The Dave Starbuck Collection

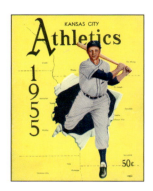 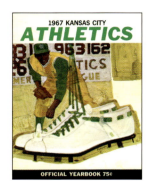

Left: A's 1955 Yearbook, their first in Kansas City
Right: A's 1967 Yearbook, their last in Kansas City
Source: The Dave Starbuck Collection

Future Royals manager Dick Howser,
during his playing days with the Kansas City Athletics
Source: The Chris Wilborn Collection

Left: Roger Maris, Kansas City A's, 1958
Center: Autographed A's bats, including the
1955 Inaugural Season bat signed by all of the players
Right: Baseball autographed by the 1958 team (including Maris)
Source: The Dave Starbuck Collection

THE LEGENDARY SATCHEL PAIGE

"Satchel Paige was the best and fastest pitcher I ever faced."
—Joe DiMaggio

Among those who pitched for the Kansas City Athletics in Municipal Stadium was the legendary Hall of Famer Satchel Paige. His last Major League game was September 25, 1965, against the Boston Red Sox. He was somewhere between 59 and 99 years old, depending upon the person you were talking to. Charlie Finley had signed Paige for the purpose of allowing him to qualify for his baseball pension. (Naturally, Finley thought he could sell a few more tickets at the same time.) Paige pitched three scoreless innings. He left the mound at the beginning of the fourth inning as the crowd sang "The Old Gray Mare" in tribute. Satchel's response was, "Age is mind over matter. If you don't mind, it don't matter."

**Left to right: A's players Johnny "Blue Moon" Odom, Jim "Catfish" Hunter,
Satchel Paige, Dick Joyce and Ron Tompkins.**
Source: The Dave Starbuck Collection

By the time Satchel Paige pitched in his last Major League game in 1965, he had already pitched in the professional ranks for thirty years. He began his professional career in 1924, pitching for the Chattanooga Black Lookouts in the Negro Leagues. After playing for other teams, he completed his career in the Negro Leagues by pitching for the Kansas City Monarchs from 1940 to 1947.

In 1948, Cleveland Indians owner Bill Veeck signed Paige to a Major League contract. At the time, he was thought to be forty-two years old, making him the oldest rookie in Major League history. He played for the Indians and the St. Louis Browns, retiring in 1953. (This occurred before Finley signed him for his one-game stint some twenty-two years later.) Paige's last professional game was with the Peninsula Grays in the Carolina League on June 21, 1966.

Satchel Paige's career spanned more than forty years. The feat was even more remarkable since his ability never waned throughout those four decades. In the words of Joe DiMaggio, Paige was "the best and fastest pitcher I ever faced."

**Left: Satchel Paige heading to the dugout after pitching
three shutout innings at the age of 59, September 25, 1965**
Source: Kansas City Star Archives
Right: Diego Seguí, who came on in relief of Satchel Paige
Source: The Chris Wilborn Collection

A 1960 payroll check for Marvin E. "Marvelous Marv" Throneberry
Source: The Dave Starbuck Collecton

Playing contracts for Johnny Lee "Blue Moon" Odom and Jose Tartabull
Source: The Dave Starbuck Collection

  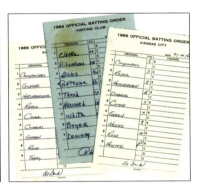

Left: Bill Starbuck's usher badge, 1960-1967
Center: A's souvenirs
Right: Managers' lineup cards from 1966
Source: The Dave Starbuck Collecton

 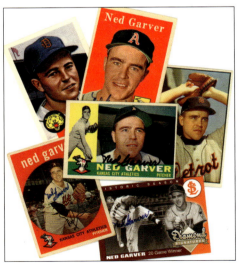

Left: Norm Siebern, first baseman Right: Ned Garver, pitcher
Source: The Dave Starbuck Collection

After the A's left for the West Coast, Kansas City was awarded a new franchise that began play in 1969. The Kansas City Royals called Municipal Stadium home until 1973, when they played their first game in the newly constructed Royals Stadium at the Harry S. Truman Sports Complex. When Lamar Hunt moved the Dallas Texans of the AFL to Kansas City, the renamed Kansas City Chiefs played their home games in Municipal Stadium from 1963 until Christmas Day in 1971. On that particular day the Chiefs lost their playoff game to the Miami Dolphins in double-overtime. It remains the longest game in NFL history. Fans were able to witness one of the greatest performances in football history, turned in by Chiefs running back Ed Podolak. In addition to the Royals and the Chiefs, the Kansas City Spurs of the North American Soccer League played their home games in the stadium from 1968 through 1970.

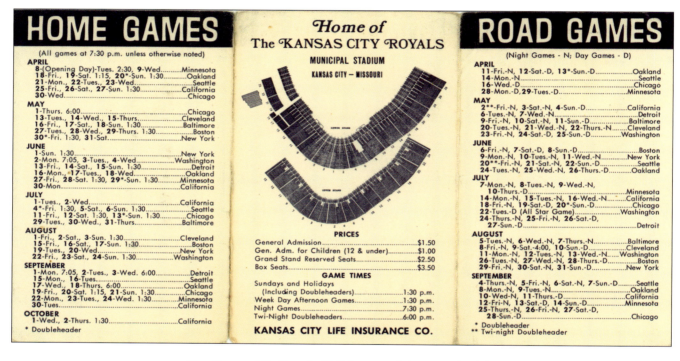

The Kansas City Royals 1969 Inaugural Season schedule
Source: The Dorri Partain Collection

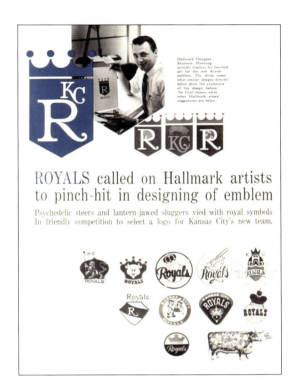

Left: Kansas City Royals logo designed by Hallmark Cards artist Shannon Manning
Source: Hallmark Cards archives
Right: Kansas City Chiefs Wolfpack promotional artwork created by
Kansas City artist John Martin, with Valentine Radford Advertising
Source: John Martin

The Beatles, you ask? On September 17, 1964, the legendary band from Liverpool performed in Municipal Stadium as part of their first United States tour. Finley had offered the band the record sum of $150,000 for a stopover in Kansas City.

Source: The Nancy Finley Collection

THE TURF ARTISTRY OF GEORGE TOMA

Teams come and go, and the stadium is gone. As I look back on my child-hood days of attending games at Municipal Stadium, I recall one vivid memory: it was reinforced each time I entered the stadium and gazed out over the immaculately maintained field. It was my own version of what a "Field of Dreams" would look like. This is the legacy of head groundskeeper George Toma, who is a master at his craft.

Left: George Toma's grounds crew shirt
Center: George Toma with Harvey the Rabbit. This photo appeared in
Sports Illustrated on June 5, 1961.
Right: The George Toma bobblehead doll
Source: The George Toma Collection

George Toma (front row, center) and his grounds crew at Municipal Stadium
Source: The George Toma Collection

MUNICIPAL STADIUM

25TH ANNIVERSARY

MUNICIPAL STADIUM WAS HOME TO THE KANSAS CITY ATHLETICS FROM 1955-67 AND THE KANSAS CITY ROYALS FROM 1969-72. THE ATHLETICS, NEWLY TRANSPLANTED FROM PHILADELPHIA, OPENED THE STADIUM APRIL 12, 1955 WITH A 6-2 WIN OVER DETROIT. AFTER THE 1967 SEASON THE ATH-LETICS MOVED TO OAKLAND, LEAVING KANSAS CITY WITHOUT BASEBALL. IN 1969, BASEBALL EXPANDED, CREATING A NEW TEAM FOR KANSAS CITY, THE ROYALS. WITH A NEW BALL-PARK NEAR COMPLETION, THE ROYALS BEAT TEXAS 4-0 IN THE FINAL GAME AT MUNICIPAL STADIUM, OCTOBER 4, 1972.

Municipal Stadium – 25th Anniversary commemorative envelope
(1972 was its last season to host MLB or NFL action)
Source: The Dave Starbuck Collection

Author's note: The Kansas City Chiefs were not the first National Football League team to call Kansas City home. In 1924, the Kansas City Blues played all their games on the road. In 1925, they played home and away games under the name of the Kansas City Cowboys. Ironically, back in 1886, a professional baseball team by that name played ball in Kansas City for two years, as members of the National League. The Cowboys were owned by Kansas City brewer Joseph Heim, Kansas City Star sports editor Jim Whitfield, and malt-and-grain entrepreneur Americus V. McKim. Whitfield ended his life by committing suicide, as a result of financial problems. McKim died a pauper and was buried in an unmarked grave at Kansas City's Elmwood Cemetery. Fortunately, the Lykins Neighborhood Association of the Society of American Baseball Researchers (SABR) placed a stone on McKim's grave, as one of the fathers of Kansas City baseball.

Azteca jersey
Source: The Steve Reyes Collection. Courtesy of Frank Salas

In 1924, Kansas City saw the emergence of the Aztecas. The team would travel to other cities in the Midwest to play against other Hispanic teams. The Aztecas won the first Mexican-American Championship tournament held in Lyons, Kansas.
- Enrique Chaurand, Kansas City Star reporter

LATINO BASEBALL AND FAST-PITCH SOFTBALL IN KANSAS CITY

Early Kansas City, Missouri, Guadalupe Centers, Inc., youth teams
Source: Guadalupe Center Collection, Kansas City Public Library

Kansas City has always been a baseball town. Not only did a Major League team play here as early as 1886 (the Kansas City Cowboys in the National League), but Little Leagues, industrial leagues, the Ban Johnson League, 3&2 Baseball, and other organizations have also emerged over the years. Today's fans can catch the action of many of these teams, in addition to the Kansas City T-Bones on the Kansas side and the World Champion Kansas City Royals at beautiful Kauffman Stadium in the Harry S. Truman Sports Complex on the Missouri side of the state line.

Baseball brought a sense of community to the many Mexican American families who settled in Argentine, Armourdale, Rosedale and in Kansas City, Missouri's West Side. Mexican immigrants came to the area to seek jobs with railroad companies, meat-packing plants, hotels, and restaurants on both sides of the state line. Families raised their children in the communities near their workplaces. As Gene T. Chávez, EdD, writes in his essay, "Pitch'em Fast Pauly: The Mexican-American Fast-Pitch Softball Leagues": "These communities engaged in hard labor, but they found time for family, friends and entertainment." As Richard Santillán expressed in *Perspectives in Mexican American Studies*, "teams and contests were far more than games for boys and girls. They involved the entire community, and they often included both cultural and political motives."

Chávez reports that Mexican Americans formed their own baseball and fast-pitch softball leagues both before and after World War II. He further states: "Mexican Americans began to form their own baseball and fast-pitch softball leagues. Many Mexican American GIs were attracted to fast-pitch softball because it was very competitive, but easier to play and fit into the community lives as they endeavored to integrate into the American mainstream and yet retain their Latino identity."

Chock-full of talent, the teams were competitive and entertaining, but they achieved notoriety for another reason. Although many teams included players capable of playing on the same level as those in the all-white Major Leagues, the Mexican American players faced the same discrimination as the Kansas City Monarchs of the Negro League. Nevertheless, as Enrique A. Chaurand reported in The Kansas City Star, "In 1924, Kansas City saw the emergence of the Aztecas. The team would travel to other cities in the Midwest to play against other Hispanic teams. The Aztecas won the first Mexican-American Championship tournament held in Lyons, Kansas."

The Aztecas, 1939
Source: The Tony Ceceña Jr. Collection

The Argentine Eagles chartered American Legion Post #213 after they were rejected from joining another "whites only" post in the Argentine district of Kansas City, Kansas. Their post, affectionately called the "Eagles' Nest," continues to operate in that Argentine community and is open to vets of all ethnic origins. Their ball field is presently under renovation and will be open for youth teams and tournaments in 2017.

**Uniforms, hats and warmup jackets for Latino teams in Kansas City,
including the Aztecas, Eagles, Pirates, Locos and Railway Ice Co.**
Source: Kansas City Museum Digital Collection (Gene T. Chávez, Curator)

Many players in the league honed their skills and longed to play on the big stage. In a 1996 article appearing in The Kansas City Star, reporter Enrique Chaurand wrote about one such player, Paul "Pauly" Hernandez, noting that although he could have played softball in any Kansas City league, a sense of tradition and community pride attracted Hernandez to the fields where his father and other relatives had once played.

"Baseball and softball at McNally Park (formerly Shawnee Park) in Kansas City, Kansas, became more than a recreational activity: it has become a way of life," Hernandez reflected. "I was raised with the game, and I knew that one day I'd be out on the same field that my dad played on. It's just tradition."

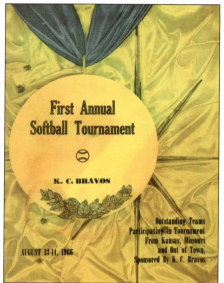
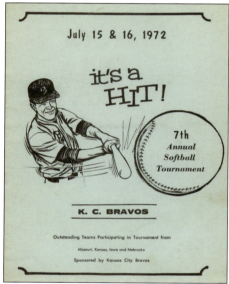
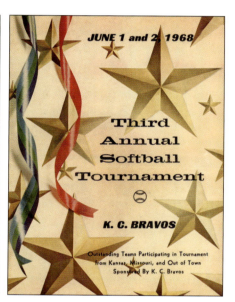

Tournament DANCE
SPONSORED BY THE BRAVOS SOFT BALL TEAM

Saturday, August 13, 1966—8 to 12 p. m.

At THE ARMORY, 18th and Ridge, K.C. Ks.

Music By THE CLEFS

Donation: Advance $2.00.   At Door $2.25

N⁰ 256

Tournament programs, trophies, and tournament dance ticket
from the Kansas City Bravos softball team

Members of the Regional Angel's Mexican-American Hall of Fame, 2015
Source: Guadalupe Centers, Inc. Collection

A Latino player with deep roots in baseball was Major League player Diego Seguí, who pitched for the Kansas City Athletics in the 1960s. Seguí, who is Cuban American, married Emily Sauceda in 1963. Her family was composed of Mexican immigrants who boasted a long line of baseball and fast-pitch stars. The Seguís raised their four children in Kansas City, Kansas. Their son David made his debut with the Baltimore Orioles in 1990, continuing to play with various Major League teams until 2004.

 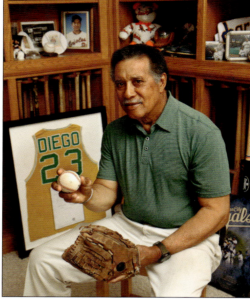 

Left: Diego and Emily (Sauceda) Seguí, 1963
Center: Bruce Mathews photo of Diego Seguí, June 2016
Right: Pioneer Award presented to Diego Seguí in 2012
from the Hispanic Heritage Baseball Museum Hall of Fame
Source, left and right: The Diego Seguí Family Collection

Kansas City Star photo of Diego Seguí coming on in relief
of the legendary Satchel Paige in Satchel's last game in a
Major League uniform, September 25, 1965
Source: The Diego Seguí Family Collection

In 1965, Charlie Finley, the flamboyant, white owner of the Oakland Athletics, brought former Negro League star Satchel Paige out of retirement to pitch three innings. At the age of fifty-nine, he would play the final Major League game in his long and glorious career. After the third inning, Paige was relieved by Seguí. Diego had seen Paige pitch when he was a young man in Cuba and was amazed by his style and effectiveness at the plate. "When I relieved the great Satchel Paige in the fourth inning of his last professional outing, I felt so honored. It will forever be a highlight of my career in baseball," reminisced Seguí. On that memorable night, on a Major League mound in Kansas City, the paths of the Mexican American Leagues, the Negro Leagues, and the Major Leagues were intertwined.

Generations of the same Hispanic families in the Kansas City area
have embraced the game of baseball.
For many it is a way of life and represents their community identity.
The K.C. Indios are in their fourth generation of Garcia family players.
Source: The Kansas City Star

As Richard Santillán wrote, "The most popular sport among Mexicans in the U.S. has been baseball. The rise of baseball as a spectator sport in the Mexican community simply reflected the rise of mass spectator sports in the nation. Nearly every Midwest Mexican community, small or large, has baseball teams to represent it. The sport became one of the major forms of recreation, and was played before overflowing crowds. Most of the teams selected names from their rich historical past, such as the *Aztécas, Mayans, Cuauhtémoc,* and *Águilas.* The choice of these names was a way of respecting and reaffirming the Mexican culture."

**A few of the trophies won by Jerry Morales
during his time as an amateur boxer in Kansas City**
Source: The Morales Family Collection

GREATER KANSAS CITY GOLDEN GLOVES

A TRIBUTE TO JERRY MORALES BY HIS SON, MARK

**Jerry Morales – 1956 Kansas City Golden Gloves Champion
112-pound weight division**
Source: The Morales Family Collection

Amateur boxing in Kansas City began in 1936 with the formation of the Greater Kansas City Golden Gloves (GKCGG) program, sponsored by The Kansas City Star. It became affiliated with other like organizations holding similar competitions throughout the United States. In 1947, the local association was reorganized by a group of prominent community-driven leaders whose goal was to improve the lives of young athletes by promoting self-confidence, sportsmanship, and physical fitness. The stewards were guided by a set of core values that would not only make these young men winners in the ring, but also successful in life. Golden Gloves was not instituted to train young men to become professional boxers; it was founded to help them develop good character.

Each Golden Gloves boxer entered competitions throughout the year, striving to represent the organization in his weight division. The young athlete then competed against champions from other states. The annual highlight was the Golden Gloves National Championship Tournament, which was held in a different location each year.

Harry S. Truman was an avid supporter of the Golden Gloves program. Encouraging our country's youth to participate in a wide variety of fitness programs was among Truman's priorities, and he served as honorary co-chairman of the Golden Gloves tournaments for more than thirty years. Other Kansas City leaders who lent their personal support to Golden Gloves included Mayors Charles B. Wheeler and Richard L. Berkley, restaurateur Carl DiCapo, radio talk show legend Mike Murphy, and Kansas City Star sports editor Ernie Mehl. Bubble Klice, Charlie Myers, Tom McHughes, Hayes Richardson, James A. DiRenna, and scores of others also lent their time, efforts, and money in support of the program.

 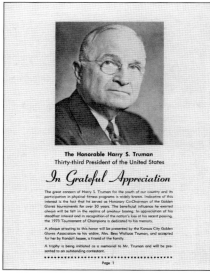 

Left: Kansas City Mayor Charles B. Wheeler welcomes participants to the 1974 National AAU Boxing Association Championship

Center: President Harry S. Truman is recognized for his more than thirty years as honorary co-chair of Greater Kansas City Golden Gloves tournaments

Right: Golden Gloves Regional Tournament Honorary Co-Chairmen Carl DiCapo and Mike Murphy

Source, all: Golden Gloves tournament programs
The Morales Family Collection

This following story is about a Kansas Citian whose entire life has revolved around Golden Gloves, first as a participant, later as a referee and coach, and finally as president of the Greater Kansas City Golden Gloves organization. The name of that ardent supporter is Jerry Morales.

Morales was raised in a close-knit family. His parents instilled in him the importance of a strong work ethic and the need for education. It was in this environment that he was introduced to amateur boxing at the Pan American Youth Boxing Club. The young man was drawn to the dedication and commitment of the boxers, and he never looked back. He became the 112-pound Kansas City Champion in 1953, 1954, and 1956.

In 1953, the Kansas City team was one of the most experienced in the country. Morales was poised to advance to an international status to compete in Europe and possibly the Olympics, should he be successful. But such good fortune was not to be. By an executive order, President Dwight Eisenhower declared that all U.S. boxers in the 1954 Olympics must number among the ranks of the military.

A young Jerry Morales with Vern and Frances Gregory, of the Whatsoever Community Center/Golden Gloves
Source: The Morales Family Collection

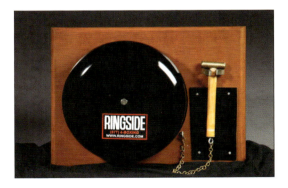

The ringside bell
Source: The Morales Family Collection

Tools of the trade
Source: The Morales Family Collection

Morales never really left the ring, even after he was no longer a participant in the action. He devoted many years giving back to the community, advocating for the health and well-being of Kansas City's youth. He continued on as an official, coach and referee in the Golden Gloves program for another fifty-five years. He also raised a family of eleven children in Kansas City's Northeast neighborhood. At the time this book was written, the eighty-two-year-old Morales and his wife were still critically involved with numerous service organizations.

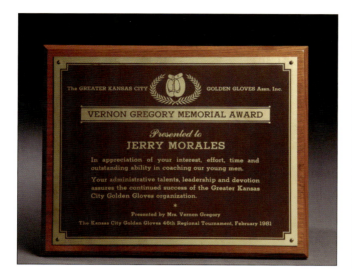

Left: In 1981, Jerry Morales was presented with the Vernon Gregory Memorial Award for his years of service to the Greater Kansas City Golden Gloves

Right: In 2001, Jerry Morales was inducted into the Kansas City Amateur Sports Hall of Champions

Source, both: The Morales Family Collection

At the 2009 Golden Gloves Tournament, Jerry Morales was cited as the outstanding official

Source: The Morales Family Collection

The Greater Kansas City Golden Gloves has hosted the National Golden Gloves Tournament a total of five times: in 1965, 1966, 1969, 1982, and 2004. Morales served as president of the Greater Kansas City Golden Gloves organization in 1982 and 2004. He was also the head referee for numerous years, and he was honored as the best referee in the city in 1974. That distinction brought with it an unusual perk: Morales was selected to referee an exhibition match at Kemper Arena featuring Muhammad Ali. On that night, Morales, the best referee in Kansas City, was charged with protecting the greatest heavyweight boxer of all time, preventing him from being cut or injured in the ring. In a twist of fate, Ali, "The Greatest," passed away on June 3, 2016, the day Morales celebrated his eighty-second birthday. The two men came from very different worlds, but they had one important thing in common: their love and passion for boxing.

Referee Jerry Morales (left) and Muhammad Ali (right)
1976 exhibition match at Kemper Arena
Source: The Kansas City Star, The Morales Family Collection

"For the Love of Boxing: A Life Devoted to Young Athletes"
Jerry Morales, referee
Source: The Kansas City Star, The Morales Family Collection

Souvenir clock given to attendees at the 1900 Priests of Pallas gala dinner
Source: The Mrs. Phil K. Weeks Collection at the Jackson County Historical Society

PRIESTS OF PALLAS

Official Program, Priests of Pallas Parade – October 5, 1892
Source: The Felicia Londré Collection

The festivities began in 1887, as a means for Kansas City to attract visitors, boost trade, stimulate the economy, and have fun while doing it. The Priests of Pallas Parade and the week-long events that accompanied it culminated in a gala ball. The parades included grand floats, first drawn by teams of horses and later by electric trolleys, which ran along the city's expansive trolley tracks. It was Kansas City's attempt to emulate New Orleans's Mardi Gras and the Veiled Prophet Fair of St. Louis. The events grew in popularity, drawing crowds of more than 500,000 people who gathered to watch the parades.

But therein lies the problem. The 1913 version of the festivities had to be cancelled, collapsing under its own weight. The floats, for example, took months to create. City services simply could not keep up with the momentum, including the demand for the electricity needed to power the clever creations. In an ironic twist, the increasing popularity of the American Royal contributed to the demise of the Priests of Pallas festivities. Later attempts to resurrect the grand ball failed to achieve the success of the original event, which ran from 1887 until 1912.

The idea for the Priests of Pallas was the brainchild of Lambdin E. Irwin, the city's first fire chief, together with a group of his fellow revelers. It became a zany and wildly popular event, in which practically the entire population of Kansas City participated. Kansas City Star staff writers Rick Montgomery and Shirl Kasper described the first parade in their 1999 book, *Kansas City: An American Story:* "On October 13, 1887, the doors of a downtown warehouse flew open. Out trotted horsemen in shiny helmets and jackets of white duck. Seventh Street soon throbbed to a parade of masked drummers, giant horse-drawn floats and a 'high priest' on an elephant. Next appeared a woman posing as Pallas Athene, the Greek Goddess of Wisdom, Science and Art. As the scene unfolded, 'Usually placid mules broke loose and scattered,' in the words of one reporter. So began the bizarre rite of fall."

William Joseph "Cable Car" Smith, reins in hand, along with parade participants including his daughter Rosa, in front of the Smith home, ready for the Priests of Pallas Parade of 1896
Source: The Anne Canfield Collection at the Jackson County Historical Society

"Castle in the Air," 1910 Priests of Pallas Parade float
Sources: Postcard from the Felicia Londré Collection
Photograph from the Jackson County Historical Society

The 1889 Priests of Pallas Gala Programme
Source: The John Herbst Collection at the Jackson County Historical Society

Left: 1910 Parade postcard; Center: 1894 Parade program; Right: 1910 Parade postcard
Sources: Left: The Tom Taylor Collection; Center: The Felicia Londré Collection
Right: The Tom Taylor Collection

Elaborate invitation to the October 4, 1889, Priests of Pallas gala
Source: The John Herbst Collection at the Jackson County Historical Society

Sample gifts presented to attendees of the Priests of Pallas gala dinners

Jewelry box – 1901
Source: The John Herbst Collection at the Jackson County Historical Society

Metal tray – 1896
Source: The Donald R. Hale Collection at the Jackson County Historical Society

Decorative plates – 1906
Source: The Felicia Londré Collection

Picture frame – 1910

Perpetual calendar – 1912

Vase - 1905

Sources: Left: The Steve Noll Collection; Center: The Jim O'Keefe Collection
Right: The John Herbst Collection at the Jackson County Historical Society

Bud vase – 1924

Oriental fan – 2007

Sample gifts from later reincarnations of the Priests of Pallas gala

Source, all: The Felicia Londré Collection

Officer's badge for the 1900 Democratic Convention
Source: The Harry S. Truman Library & Museum

KANSAS CITY'S NATIONAL POLITICAL CONVENTIONS

THE DEMOCRATIC NATIONAL CONVENTION OF 1900
July 4 – 6, 1900

Kansas City's first Convention Hall (before the fire)
Source: The Gloria Dobbs and Courtney Sloan Collection

Kansas City's first Convention Hall (after the fire)
Source: Missouri Valley Special Collections, Kansas City Public Library

The 1900 Democratic National Convention marked the culmination of a remarkable ninety-day period filled with tragedy, perseverance and ultimately, the innate human ability to overcome adversity. Those ninety days represent a shining example of the indomitable "Kansas City Spirit." While it is not unique to any one group of human beings, it does define us—who we are, where we came from, and where we are headed. We embrace and exemplify that spirit.

By 1900, Kansas City had become one of the most desirable convention locations in the country. Centrally situated and easily accessible by train from either coast, Kansas City was the perfect venue to host any large gathering. Ample hotel rooms had been built, and the city had just completed construction of a 20,000-seat convention hall in 1899. It was among the largest such facilities in the United States. As the city embarked on a new century, it also landed the rights to host the 1900 Democratic National Convention, which was set to convene on July 3, 1900. But the unthinkable happened on the afternoon of April 3, when flames consumed the brand-new convention hall. It burned to the ground in a mere thirty minutes. Although an official cause was never determined, it was thought to be of a suspicious nature. Only ninety days remained before the Democrats would commence their event: the clock was ticking.

Delegates in their seats in the second Convention Hall
Source: Missouri Valley Special Collections, Kansas City Public Library

Exterior view of the second Convention Hall
Source: The Steve Noll Collection

Did the city throw up its hands in defeat? Was the convention moved to another city that coveted the economic boost that was certain to follow? Absolutely not! City fathers convinced the conventioneers that the hall could be rebuilt, allowing the event to be held in Kansas City as though nothing had happened. Miraculously, every event took place as planned.

William Jennings Bryan secured the nomination, and Adlai E. Stevenson became his running mate. Since Stevenson had just served as vice-president, he was actually running to retain his position. The selection of Stevenson as the vice-presidential candidate brought great division to the Democratic

William Jennings Bryan
Democratic Presidential Nominee

Adlai E. Stevenson
Democratic Vice-Presidential Nominee

Source, both: Library of Congress

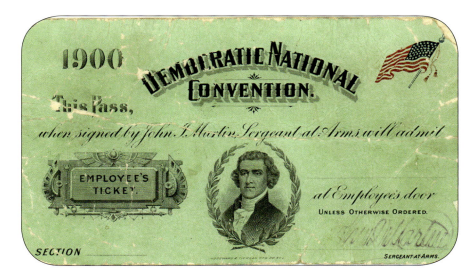

Left: Bryan/Stevenson campaign badge
Source: The Harry S. Truman Library & Museum
Right: Employee ticket to enter Convention Hall
Source: Missouri Valley Special Collections, Kansas City Public Library

Party. In the general election, the duo lost out to the Republican ticket of William McKinley and Theodore Roosevelt. McKinley, the last Civil War veteran to be elected to the presidency, was assassinated six months after he took office. Roosevelt thereby became the president of the United States.

A number of firsts characterized the 1900 Convention. It was the first time a woman was chosen as a delegate. Elizabeth Cohen, of Salt Lake City, Utah, substituted as an alternate when one of the male delegates was unable to serve. Cohen was given the honor of seconding the nomination of William Jennings Bryan. The convention also witnessed the first royal to attend a convention: the honor went to David Kawānanakoa, representing the Kingdom of Hawaii, the United States' newest territory. Of local note, the young Harry S. Truman participated as a page.

Guest ticket for the 1900 Democratic National Convention
Source: Missouri Valley Special Collections, Kansas City Public Library

THE REPUBLICAN NATIONAL CONVENTION OF 1928
June 12 – 15, 1928

**Delegates gathering at Convention Hall for the second day
of the 1928 Republican National Convention**
Source: Missouri Valley Special Collections, Kansas City Public Library

**Commerce Secretary Herbert Hoover (left)
Chosen at the 1928 Convention as the Republican candidate for President
Senate Majority Leader Charles Curtis of Kansas (right) rounded out the ticket**
Source, both: Library of Congress

Convening in the same hall that the Democrats had used in 1900, Herbert Hoover and his running mate, Charles Curtis (Senate majority leader from Kansas), received their party's nomination. President Coolidge had surprisingly announced that he would not seek re-election. From this springboard, Hoover eventually succeeded to the nation's highest elective office. He was elected to lead the nation in one of its most difficult eras, the Great Depression.

From day one of the convention, the presence of Kansas City was evident in the invocations given by prominent local clergy. On June 12, the opening prayer was offered by Bishop S. C. Partridge of the Episcopal Diocese of Western Missouri. Catholic Bishop Thomas F. Lillis opened the proceedings on June 13. He was followed on June 14 by Rabbi Herman M. Cohen of the Congregation Keneseth-Israel Beth Shalom, Kansas City, Missouri. The honor of delivering the invocation on the fifteenth, the convention's last day, went to Bishop E. L. Waldorf of the Methodist Episcopal Diocese of Kansas City. Newspaper accounts reported that Bishop Waldorf prayed for "the blessings of God for the man who had been given the great place by this convention."

Left: Telephone Messenger badge
Center: Kansas City Host Committee badge issued to Harry S. Truman
Right: Convention Executive badge
Source, all: The Harry S. Truman Library & Museum

With the Great Depression looming, Hoover would need all the prayers he could get. In a campaign circular published after the convention, Hoover promised "to put a chicken in every pot and a car in every garage." In the end, Hoover received more than fifty-eight percent of the popular vote. His opponent, Al Smith, four-term Democratic governor from New York, received slightly less than forty-one percent.

Left: Promotional material for the 1928 Republican Convention
Center: Admittance card for telephone messenger
Right: Credentials for Asst. Sergeant-at-Arms
Source: Missouri Valley Special Collections, Kansas City Public Library

The Kansas City Republican Convention of 1928 went off without a hitch, minus the drama that had led up to the previous convention in 1900. But like the convention of 1900, the Republicans of 1928 were drawn to the "Kansas City Spirit." It would be the last convention held in the hall. In 1935, the building was demolished and replaced by the architectural treasure, Municipal Auditorium.

THE REPUBLICAN CONVENTION OF 1976
August 16 – 19, 1976

Left: President Gerald Ford, First Lady Betty Ford, Vice-President Nelson Rockefeller, and vice-presidential candidate Bob Dole celebrate winning the nomination at the Republican Convention, Kansas City, Missouri.
Source: Library of Congress, John T. Bledsoe, photo
Right: Ford supporters on the convention floor
Source, right: Library of Congress

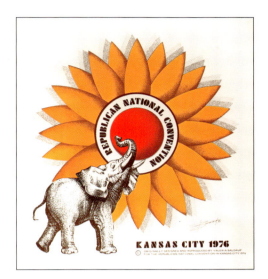 

Left: Advertising artwork for the 1976 Republican Convention Right: Host committee badges
Source, both: The Anita Gorman Collection

The decision to hold the 1976 Republican Convention in Kansas City was not an easy one. There were major concerns about the proposed location of Kemper Arena, situated in the city's undeveloped West Bottoms. The arena was rather isolated, some distance from major hotels. That problem brought about another major issue: untested public transportation. But in typical Kansas City fashion, those concerns were put to rest, beginning with the success of the smoothly running pre-convention activities. With earlier problems satisfactorily addressed, the convention soon turned to the business at hand: selecting the party's presidential and vice-presidential nominees.

The incumbent, Leslie Lynch King Jr. (aka Gerald Ford), was favored to win the nomination, although support for Ronald Reagan was beginning

Left: President Gerald R. Ford Right: Kansas Senator Robert Dole

to emerge. During the convention, Ford succeeded in winning the nomination: Ronald Reagan would have to wait his turn. Ford chose Kansas Senator Bob Dole as his running mate. Dole was certainly the local favorite. Gerald Ford had been sworn into the highest elected office in the land when President Richard Nixon resigned during the Watergate scandal. From the Kansas City Convention, Ford would go on to lose the general election to Democrat Jimmy Carter.

At the close of the last session, Kansas Citians Dick and Janet Rees walked the convention floor in search of discarded treasures. In Dick's own words, some forty years later: "We both recognized the significance of the historical aspect of the convention being held in KC and felt that it probably wouldn't happen again in the remainder of our lifetimes. With both of us being saver/collectors, we wanted to preserve at least a small part of the history, then figure out what to do with it many years later.

"Speaking also for my late wife, I'm pleased that we were able to salvage the quantity that we did, of a broad range of items simply left on the floor in a vacant Kemper Arena after the convention ended. We realized at the time that we obtained some very unique items that might well not be preserved elsewhere."

EMBARGOED FOR RELEASE   AUGUST 19, 1976
UPON DELIVERY

Office of the White House Press Secretary
(Kansas City, Missouri)
----------------------   ----------------------

THE WHITE HOUSE

TEXT OF THE PRESIDENT'S ACCEPTANCE ADDRESS
AS PREPARED FOR DELIVERY BEFORE
THE 1976 REPUBLICAN NATIONAL CONVENTION

KEMPER ARENA
KANSAS CITY, MISSOURI

Delegates and Alternates to this Republican Convention: I am honored by your nomination -- and I accept it.

I accept with pride, with gratitude, and with a total will to win a great victory for the American people.

We will wage a winning campaign in every region of this country -- from the snowy banks of Minnesota to the sandy plains of Georgia.

We concede not a single state. We concede not a single vote.

This evening I am proud to stand before this convention as the first incumbent President since Dwight D. Eisenhower who can tell the American people: America is at peace.

Tonight I can tell you straight away --
This nation is sound.
This nation is secure.
This nation is on the march to full economic recovery and a better quality of life for all Americans.

I am deeply grateful to those who stood with me in winning the nomination of the party whose cause I have served all my adult life.

I respect the convictions of those who want a change in Washington. I want a change, too. After 22 long years of majority misrule, let's change the United States Congress.

My gratitude tonight reaches far beyond this arena, to countless friends whose confidence, hard work, and unselfish support have brought me to this moment.

It would be unfair to single out anyone. But may I make an exception for my wonderful family, Mike, Jack, Steve and Susan -- and especially my

---

MY FELLOW REPUBLICANS -- MY FELLOW AMERICANS.

I STAND BEFORE YOU TONIGHT PROUD OF THE CONFIDENCE OUR PRESIDENT HAS SHOWN IN ME, GRATIFIED BY YOUR TRUST, HUMBLED BY THIS NEW OPPORTUNITY TO SERVE THE NATION WE LOVE, AND DETERMINED TO WORK WITH ALL MY HEART TO INSURE FOUR MORE YEARS OF REPUBLICAN LEADERSHIP IN THE WHITE HOUSE.

PRESIDENT FORD'S ADMINISTRATION BEGAN WITH A PRAYER. TRUSTING IN A JUST AND BENEFICIENT GOD, AND IN THE COURAGE AND WISDOM AND GOOD WILL OF OUR PEOPLE, THE PRESIDENT ACCEPTED STEWARDSHIP OF OUR NATION IN ONE OF THE MOST DIFFICULT TIMES IN OUR HISTORY.

WITH THE HELP OF GOD, WITH THE GOOD WILL OF OUR PEOPLE, AND WITH HIS OWN COURAGE, COMPASSION AND WISDOM, AMERICA HAS WEATHERED THE STORM.

TODAY, THERE ARE THOSE WHO TELL AMERICANS TO LOWER THEIR EXPECTATIONS. AMERICA WAS NOT BUILT BY MEN AND WOMEN WITH LIMITED VISION AND SMALL HOPES AND LOW EXPECTATIONS.

IT WAS BUILT BY MEN AND WOMEN WITH TOMORROW ON THEIR MINDS. IT WAS BUILT BY BELIEVERS -- BY THOSE WHO COULD LOOK ACROSS THE BROAD SWEEP OF A BOUNTEOUS LAND OF UNBOUNDED OPPORTUNITY AND SEE POSSIBILITIES NONE BEFORE HAD EVER EVEN DREAMED OF.

IN THEIR EYES, THE FUTURE GLEAMED BRIGHTLY, AND UPON THEIR ACHIEVEMENTS WE LIVE TODAY -- WITH MORE FREEDOM, MORE OPPORTUNITY, MORE DIGNITY, MORE WEALTH AND WITH GREATER OBLIGATIONS, THAN ANY PEOPLE BEFORE IN HISTORY.

MY FELLOW REPUBLICANS -- WE NEED NOT ASK THE AMERICAN PEOPLE TO LOWER THEIR EXPECTATIONS.

Left: President Ford's acceptance speech Right: Sen. Dole's acceptance speech
Source, both: The Dick and Janet Lee Rees Collection

**Kemper Arena, Kansas City, Missouri, ready for the
1976 Republican National Convention**
Source: The Chris Wilborn Collection

Memories from the 1976 Republican National Convention
Source: The Dick and Janet Lee Rees Collection

Information has been received which indicates that your son
is now interned as a prisoner of war by the German
Government at Stalag Luft 1, Germany

—Howard F. Bresee, Col., Director,
American Prisoner of War Information Bureau

POW MEDAL

Awarded to Lt. Fred H. Olander Jr.
For honorable service while a prisoner of war
The United States of America
Source: The Mina Steen Collection

LT. FREDERIC HERBERT OLANDER JR.

WORLD WAR II POW

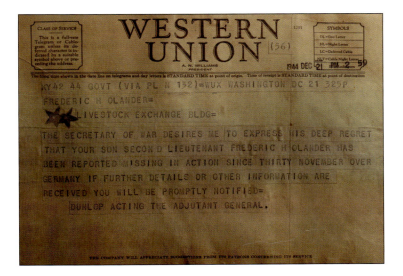

MISSING IN ACTION TELEGRAM
to Frederic H. Olander
Livestock Exchange Building

The Secretary of War desires me to express his deep regret
that your son Second Lieutenant Frederic Olander has
been reported Missing in Action since 31 November over Germany.
if further details or other information are received
you will be promptly notified.

Dunlop Acting Adjutant General
Source: The Mina Steen Collection

Fred Olander Jr. was born in Kansas City, graduated from Border Star Grade School, Southwest High School, and the University of Kansas. He was a member of the "Greatest Generation," exhibiting the character traits of a strong work ethic and a devotion to God and country. He came by them honestly. His grandfather, John W. Olander, was one of the earliest livestock commission merchants in Kansas City. It was a hard and dirty business, but it was also a profession that built character. His father, Fred Olander Sr., served honorably in World War I. Afterward, Fred Sr. embarked upon a long career in the livestock business. He rose to become the youngest person ever elected to serve as president of the Kansas City Livestock Exchange, a position to which he was twice elected. In an interesting coincidence, upon his return from the war, Fred Sr. met and married Mary

Colmery, whose father, Harry W. Colmery, had recently authored and lobbied for the successful passage of the Servicemen's Readjustment Act of 1944 (aka "the GI Bill"). Fred Jr. shared much more information about the meaning of that bill and what it did for him and other veterans than he did about his experiences as a POW. His daughter, Mina Steen, has supported decades-long efforts by veterans who have sought to see Colmery awarded the Presidential Medal of Freedom for his service to the country.

 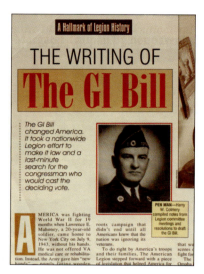 

**Left: Fred Olander Sr. in France during World War I (father of Lt. Fred Olander Jr.)
Center and Right: Harry Colmery, WWI veteran and author of GI Bill**
Source: The Mina Steen Collection

2nd Lt. Frederic Herbert Olander Jr.
Source: The Mina Steen Collection

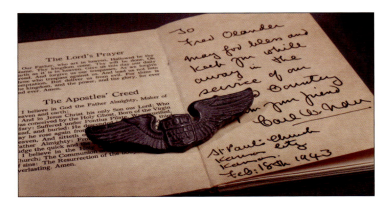

Prayer book from Rev. Carl W. Nau to Fred Olander Jr.
St. Paul's Episcopal Church, Kansas City, Kansas
Presented February 18, 1943
Source: The Mina Steen Collection

During World War II Fred Olander Jr. rose to the rank of Second Lieutenant and served in the Eighth Air Force as a navigator aboard a B-17. The plane and crew made twenty-seven successful missions, the final one of which ended in his capture by the German army. Olander was a POW from November 30, 1944, until May 1, 1945; his plane had been struck and forced down behind enemy lines. Remarkably, he chronicled the incident in his wartime diary: "November 30, 1944: After being pretty well hit over Merseburg, we bailed out over Heiligenstadt, where the Gestapo kept us in a small jail overnight. Took all personal items and no treatment for the slight head wound I had received from flak." After many days of travel, Fred and his twenty-three fellow prisoners arrived at the POW camp, Stalag Luft 1 Barth, Germany, where they would spend the final six months of the war. The men managed to keep their sense of humor, dubbing themselves "The Blasphemous 24 of Block 307, Room 3."

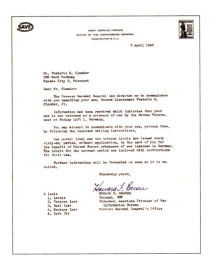

American Prisoner of War Information Bureau letter, 3 April 1945
Source: The Mina Steen Collection

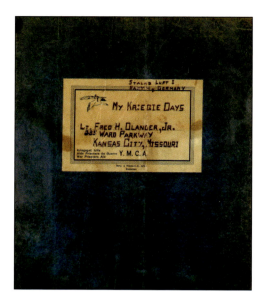
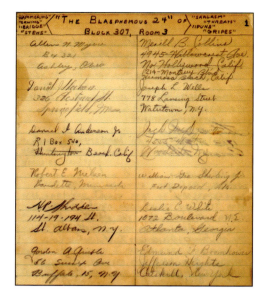
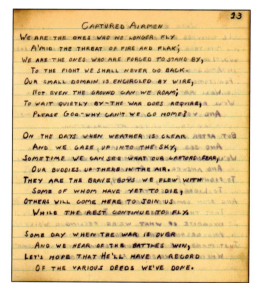

Excerpts from the POW diary of Lt. Frederic H. Olander Jr.
Source: The Mina Steen Collection

Lt. Olander and his cellmates were treated fairly in the closing days of the war, although they suffered from a lack of adequate food and water. But as news from the war trickled into the camp, it became clear that the Germans were resigned to the fact that they faced defeat. They greatly feared reprisals after the war, if the Allied Forces found that they had treated the prisoners poorly.

On May 1, 1945, Olander awoke to the news that Allied soldiers had taken over the towers guarding the camp: the "Blasphemous 24" were no longer captives. He entered the following excerpt in his diary: "At 10:23, as we were listening to the Hit Parade thru BBG, we were told that advance forces of Russians had come in camp and we were liberated. Great shouting.

Then the news told of Hitler's death. What a May Day. Topped off by the National Anthem at 11:15 p.m."

Years later, after watching the movie *Saving Private Ryan,* Olander composed a letter to a friend in which he expressed his thoughts. In perhaps an unintentional reflection of his own wartime experiences, he wrote: "The theme is of a group of soldiers led by a Captain who had become a strong military leader after being a college English professor. The group's charge was to find Private Ryan, who was on the front lines in France during World War II, and bring him safely back so that he could be sent home with an honorable discharge, as three of his brothers had already been lost in combat. In fulfilling their charge the group did go through war's hell many times, and just as Private Ryan was to be saved the Captain was wounded mortally. In his final words the Captain asked Private Ryan 'to lead a good life.' The concluding scene of the poignant movie is in one of the military graveyards in France at the grave of the Captain. The then elderly Private Ryan turns to his wife, Mary, and says, as a question, 'I have led a good life, haven't I?' I'm pretty sure there comes a time in every sincere person's life when they will ask that same question of someone. I hope that these words answer the question if asked of us. God bless you and yours, Fred."

After World War II, Olander made his career in the steel industry. Among the many community organizations blessed by his support and talents were the American Royal, which he served as governor, and Saint Luke's Hospital, which he served for twenty years as a board member and chairman of the Ethical Concerns Committee.

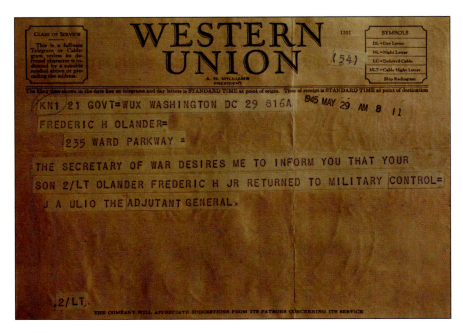

POW RELEASE TELEGRAM
2/Lt. Frederic H. Olander Jr. – May 29, 1945, 8:11 a.m.
Source: The Mina Steen Collection

The Bronze Star for Heroic Action awarded to
Pvt. Daniel DiSalvo Sr.
Source: The Daniel DiSalvo Jr. Collection

Of all the collections we amass over the years, none represent more poignant stories than the medals earned during wartime and handed down from father to son. We share the experiences of a few in honor of the many who served. Kansas Citians can boast many achievements, but their hard-won medals shine in a category of their own.

PVT. DANIEL DISALVO SR.

WORLD WAR II

  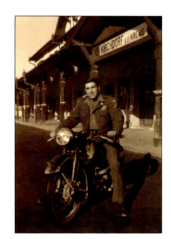

Daniel DiSalvo Sr., WWII
Source: The Daniel DiSalvo Jr. Collection

The American soldiers who served during World War II came from all walks of life, but they shared a sense of purpose and pride. Those who returned home safely as well as those who did not were all members of the "Greatest Generation." That title is their badge of honor. The soldiers were not in it for the glory; they felt it was their duty to serve their country. It was simply their responsibility, no questions asked. They served with a sense of humility rarely seen since.

Another similarity among their ranks was the fact that many patriots preferred not to discuss their wartime experiences. Perhaps they did not wish to recollect the horrors of battle; or perhaps they simply viewed their service as a necessary task that was long past.

Daniel DiSalvo Sr. was a member of that great generation. Before being called to duty at the age of eighteen years and seven months, he worked as a welder in a war plant. His military orders took him and other members of the 29th Division to France, Luxembourg, Germany and Czechoslovakia. DiSalvo saw it all, and in so doing he became one of the most decorated draftees of the war. In total he received eight citations, all earned before his twenty-first birthday: the European-African Campaign Medal with four major battle stars that included the Battle of Hill 310, the Battle of Northern France, the Battle of the Bulge at Ardennes (in which his unit emerged at only twenty percent of the strength it had going in), and the Battle of the Rhineland; the World War II Army of Occupation Medal for his service as a guard in a German POW camp during 1945-1946 in Munich; the World War II Army Infantry Combat Medal (a result of serving 210 days in combat and clean-up action in towns that had been occupied by the Germans); the World War II Bronze Star for heroic action in a daylight patrol where he served as point man on many occasions; the World War II Victory Medal; the World War II French Liberation Medal, specifically for the liberation of Paris; the Good Conduct Medal; and the Missouri Veterans Medal. The hero's son, Daniel DiSalvo Jr., inherited the collection, which holds an honored place in his heart and home.

Daniel Sr. was among the veterans who found it difficult to talk about the war, and his family learned to allow him to discuss his experiences in his own time. Daniel Jr. recalls one particular story his father loved to tell in later life: "[My father] and another [American] soldier were on a prisoner detail to escort sixteen German soldiers back behind the front lines. My dad was leading the way in the front and the other soldier was in the rear. All of a sudden, the soldier in the rear yelled at my dad to get out of the way, because he was going to kill all of the prisoners. My dad yelled back at him, 'No! The war is over for these men; they are just old men and boys.' He knew then that he did the right thing by stopping the other soldier from killing those men. It was a conviction he took with him to his own grave. When they started walking, one of the prisoners told my dad that the SS officer ahead of him had a pistol in his boot! My dad brought the pistol home from the war. He often wondered what his and the other soldier's lives would have been like had they killed the prisoners."

Daniel Jr. concluded: "My dad would ask many times, 'Why was I spared? There are better men than me in the ground over there.'" It's a question that none of us can answer in this lifetime.

MEDALS AND CITATIONS EARNED BY DANIEL DISALVO SR. DURING WORLD WAR II

26th Division – Yankee Division Army Shoulder Epaulet   European-African Campaign Medal

Army of Occupation Medal   **French Liberation Medal**

Good Conduct Medal   **Victory Medal**   **Missouri Veterans Medal**

Army Combat Medal
Source, all: The Daniel DiSalvo Jr. Collection

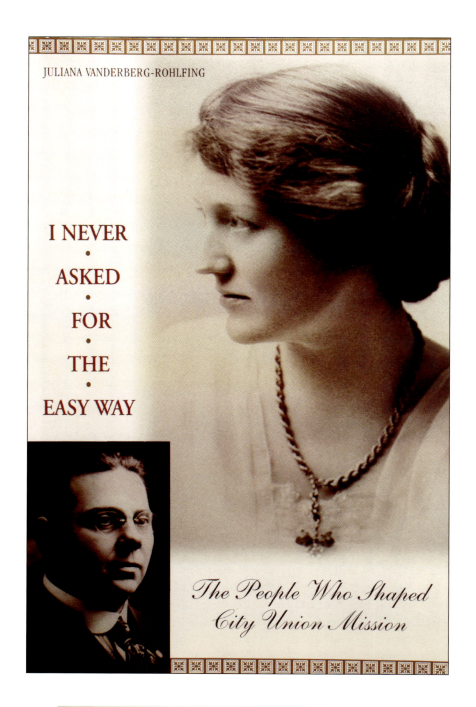

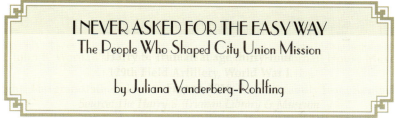

I NEVER ASKED FOR THE EASY WAY
The People Who Shaped City Union Mission

by Juliana Vanderberg-Rohlfing

GOD'S HUMAN SPARROWS

THE WORK OF CITY UNION MISSION

**The Rev. David Bulkley and his wife, Beulah,
founders of City Union Mission**
Source: The Bulkley-Vanderberg Family Collection

The Roaring Twenties were not lost on Kansas City. Our town boasted Fairyland Park, a new baseball stadium at Twenty-second Street and Brooklyn, jazz at Eighteenth Street and Vine, radio programs, talking movies, and all-night dance marathons. The early and mid-1920s were a time of great prosperity in Kansas City. But there was also blight on the urban landscape, caused by segregation, discrimination, and a growing disparity between the classes.

In this environment the Rev. David Bulkley and his wife, Beulah, embarked on a lifelong mission to rescue "God's Human Sparrows"—the minister's term for the unfortunate citizens living in poverty and hopelessness. The couple set out to serve the very dregs of society, those whose lives were plagued by crime, drunkenness, and prostitution. They established City Union Mission in 1924, which provided nourishing meals for homeless men. Their charges soon expanded to include women, children, and entire families. The Bulkleys welcomed everyone who came to them.

Scotty, helped by City Union Mission
On the reverse side of the photo are these words:
"Scotty, old and only in the way."
Source: The Bulkley-Vanderberg Family Collection

Dan Doty, executive director of City Union Mission, likened the Bulkleys' mission to that of the Lord. 'David,' Bulkley asked, 'Does God care about homeless people?'

"He then asked, 'When was the last time you contemplated a sparrow?' He was referring to the twelfth chapter of Luke, verses six and seven, in which Jesus teaches that God does not forget a sparrow falling to the ground. If God cares about sparrows, how much greater value do His human creations have in His eyes? These forgotten men, women and children are God's human sparrows. He does not forget them. We shouldn't either."

The well-used Bibles of Beulah and David Bulkley
Source: The Bulkley-Vanderberg Family Collection

Entries made by Beulah Bulkley in her daily journal
Source: The Bulkley-Vanderberg Family Collection

**A letter dated November 3, 1924, from Dr. E. A. Reeves to David and Beulah Bulkley,
written after providing medical assistance to Beulah**
Source: The Bulkley-Vanderberg Family Collection

Mr. & Mrs. Bulkley
Kansas City, Mo.
Dear Friends: After what I saw last night of your work and service,
and sacrifice I feel impelled to mail to you the enclosed.
I cannot ask you to be indebted to me when you are doing what you are
for the cause. Please accept this in the spirit in which it is offered and
if I can help or serve you in the future, please call on me.
Very Sincerely,
Dr. E.A. Reaves

Eventually, the torch was passed to the Bulkleys' daughter Ruth and her husband, Maurice Vanderberg. Today, the work is carried on by Dan Doty, the staff of City Union Mission, and the thousands of volunteers who have committed their own lives to helping "the least among us."

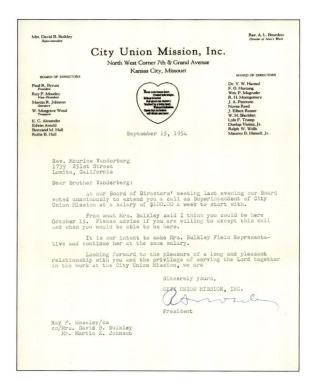

Letter of September 15, 1954, from the Board of Directors of City Union Mission to Rev. Maurice Vanderberg extending the call to serve as superintendent of the mission
Source: The Bulkley-Vanderberg Family Collection

Volunteers made quilts for Tot Lot, a camp started by Mrs. Bulkley in the early 1930s for three-to-six-year-old children
Source: The Bulkley-Vanderberg Family Collection

IT'S NEVER TOO LATE FOR REDEMPTION

The story of the Bulkleys and the early days of City Union Mission would not be complete without reflecting on their relationship with one of Kansas City's more notorious madams, Annie Chambers.

Annie ran a brothel in the same block as the establishments of Eva Prince and Madame Lovejoy, at Third Street and Wyandotte Street. Madame Lovejoy's pleasure palace was purchased by the Bulkleys, who renamed it "Harbor House." The couple resided there, among the forgotten residents whose lives and souls they were working to save. In 1933, one of Annie's "girls" asked Bulkley to preside over her infant daughter's funeral. Annie, then ninety-three, was so moved by the minister's words that she turned her life over to Christ and gave the mother and child her own home to advance the work of the mission. In her own words, Annie remarked: "Isn't it strange that in this house where so many women have led a life so far from what was right, now I, the worst of them all, have turned the place into a mission for the saving of just such women and am preaching to them the gospel of salvation?" Annie died two years later, proving once again that it is never too late for redemption.

Left: Annie Chambers at age 92 in front of the house she gave to City Union Mission
Right: Annie Chambers, third from left, front row – the CUM Sewing Club
Source: The archives of City Union Mission

CARRIE WESTLAKE WHITNEY
"The Mother of Kansas City's Public Library System"

She is the smartest woman I've ever known.

—James M. Greenwood
Superintendent of Schools, 1874-1913

THE KANSAS CITY PUBLIC LIBRARY

THE EARLY YEARS

Carrie Westlake Whitney became Kansas City's first public librarian in 1881. She served in that capacity for nearly thirty more years, from the library's infancy to its mature status as the recipient of national acclaim. She was well-loved by the library patrons, especially the children. During her tenure the collection of books grew from a meager one thousand to more than one hundred thousand. In her own words, she penned what might be considered her epitaph: "Mrs. Whitney's biography is the history of the Kansas City Public Library." Her own life and the early life of the library were inseparable. Whitney's time as director saw the library grow from a small space that also housed the office of the Board of Education to an independent building at Eighth Street and Oak Street. In 1898, the Board of Education built a magnificent edifice at Ninth Street and Locust Street, to house the growing library collection. The building stands as a treasure designed by Board of Education architects William F. Hackney and Charles A. Smith, with architect Adriance Van Brunt acting as a consultant.

**The first library cabinet from the office of James M. Greenwood,
now located on the lobby level of the Central Library at 14 West Tenth Street**
Source: Kansas City Public Library

Carrie Whitney was elected president of the Missouri Library Association. She was also an active member of the American Library Association. A prolific author, she wrote numerous articles concerning the need for higher-quality library books for children, her favorite patrons. But she is best remembered for her epic three-volume series titled *Kansas City, Missouri: Its History and Its People 1808-1908*. Whitney was keenly aware of the important roles the area's early residents had in shaping Kansas City. She did not want the stories of their accomplishments to become lost to future generations.

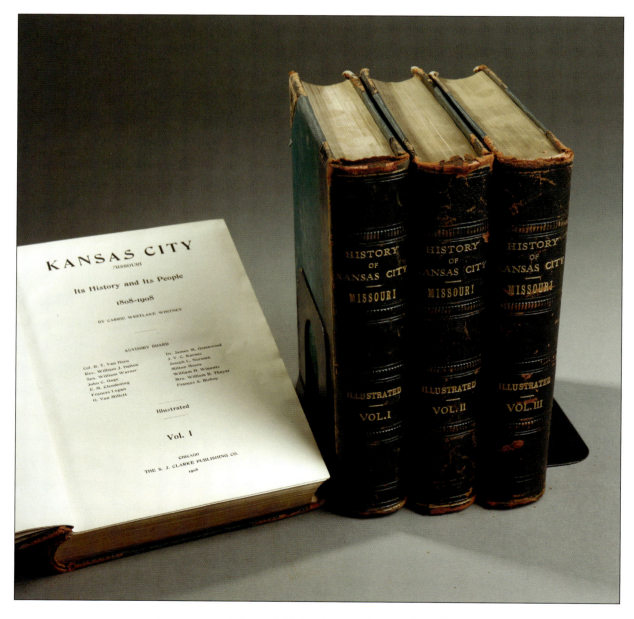

Kansas City, Missouri: Its History and Its People 1808-1908
by Carrie Westlake Whitney
Source: Missouri Valley Special Collections, Kansas City Public Library

**Index cards for works by Carrie Westlake Whitney contained in a
card cabinet from the Kansas City Public Library at Ninth Street and Locust Street**
Source: Missouri Valley Special Collections, Kansas City Public Library

In the end, however, Whitney's efforts and accomplishments could not overcome the infighting taking place among members of the politically divided Board of Education. She was demoted to assistant librarian in 1910; and by 1912, she was "deposed," in the words of the Kansas City Journal. The Journal further reported: "The board concluded that the position should be held by a man."

At the time of Whitney's death in 1934, The Kansas City Star described her life in this manner: "Her fine capacity for the office of librarian was quickened by a love of books and an unusual discrimination in literary values. There were many regrets, publicly and privately expressed, when she 'retired.' Mrs. Whitney enjoyed her contacts during her days at the library, but service was her first consideration, and it was this consideration that caused her to suggest to the Board of Education the establishing of branch libraries and the inauguration of a children's department."

After her so-called retirement, Whitney lived a very private life, out of public view. According to a 1934 article in The Kansas City Star: "She and her inseparable friend and assistant librarian, Miss Frances A. Bishop, already had cast their lot together. For more than forty years these two, bound by a rare and beautiful friendship, found happiness in each other and the books and current literature with which they surrounded themselves."

James M. Greenwood, who served as Superintendent of Public Schools of Kansas City, Missouri, from 1874 until 1913, was among those who appreciated and supported Whitney. Greenwood's time in that office coincided with Whitney's tenure as librarian. Despite a simmering opposition to public schools, Greenwood worked tirelessly to increase daily attendance. At that time, no regulations made attendance mandatory. Both civic leaders understood the values to be gained from education. Like Whitney, Greenwood championed education on a national level, serving as president of the National Education Association in 1898. Greenwood is also known as the founder of the Kansas City Library.

James Greenwood's accomplishments in the advancement of education in Kansas City were many. He promoted a system of learning from kindergarten to graduate school. He initiated night classes for those who worked during the day. He introduced laboratory classes for scientific study. He initiated merit-based hiring practices, and he actively promoted the hiring and advancement of women in all areas of education.

Left: James M. Greenwood, Superintendent of Public Schools of Kansas City, Missouri
Right: Chair dedicated to Mr. James M. Greenwood in recognition of his
service to education in Kansas City
Source: Kansas City Public Library

George Sheidley also deserves recognition for the success of the library in its infancy. In 1894, two years before his death, Sheidley made a generous donation to the library for the purpose of expanding its collection. His twenty-five-thousand-dollar gift enabled the library to increase its number of volumes from thirty thousand to forty thousand.

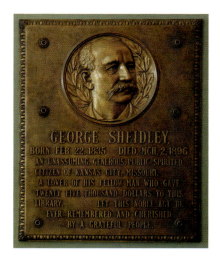

GEORGE SHEIDLEY
1835-1896
An unassuming, generous and public-spirited citizen of Kansas City, Missouri.
A lover of his fellow man who gave twenty-five thousand dollars to this library.
Let this noble act be ever remembered and cherished by a grateful people.
A plaque located in the lobby of the Kansas City Public Library, 14 West Tenth Street

Sheidley had come to Kansas City in the 1870s. The entrepreneur soon amassed a fortune in excess of one million dollars. The highly regarded owner of the Sheidley Cattle Company, he was also a stockholder in the Kansas City Cable Company and a significant real estate investor. Sheidley was well-known for his public spirit and philanthropy.

THE KANSAS CITY PUBLIC LIBRARY AT NINTH STREET AND LOCUST STREET
1898 -1960

The Kansas City Public Library in 1909
Ninth Street and Locust Street
Source: Library of Congress

Adult and Children's Reading Rooms at Ninth Street and Locust Street
Source, both: Missouri Valley Special Collections, Kansas City Public Library

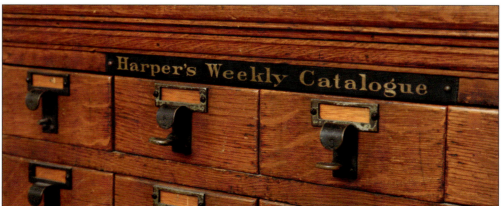

Card catalogues used at the Kansas City Public Library, Ninth Street and Locust Street
Source: Kansas City Public Library

**Left: Letter from Carrie Westlake Whitney to the Board of Education,
requesting the purchase of a Hammond typewriter for the library,
dated January 19, 1888
Right: A circa 1915 model of the Hammond typewriter used at the Ninth Street and Locust Street location**
Source, both: Missouri Valley Special Collections, Kansas City Public Library

*"In Kansas City, when I first became seriously interested in cartooning, I gained my first
information on animation from a book written by H.C. Lutz which I procured from
the Kansas City Public Library. I feel the Public Library has been a very definite help
to me all through my career."*

—Walt Disney, August 27, 1937

1937 letter from Walt Disney to the Kansas City Public Library
Source: Missouri Valley Special Collections, Kansas City Public Library

The Ozark National Life Building, Ninth Street and Locust Street, 2016
(formerly the Kansas City Public Library, 1898-1960)

The Charles A. Smith-designed library has always been a beautiful building, serving as Kansas City's main library for more than sixty years. Today, the building serves as private office space. The early pioneers of the library system took great pride in its early accomplishments. Col. Thomas H. Swope lay in state in its magnificent rotunda following his untimely death in 1909. His coffin, draped in black, was placed between two massive marble columns. The building was not only home to the library, but also a civic center and gathering place. The second floor housed William Rockhill Nelson's Western Gallery of Art, forerunner to the Nelson-Atkins Museum of Art.

THE FOURTH LIBRARY BUILDING, FROM TWELFTH STREET TO THIRTEENTH STREET AND MCGEE STREET TO OAK STREET

In 1956, the voters of Kansas City approved a $6 million bond package to provide for an even larger library. As circulation had reached three million the new library was dedicated in July of 1960. While the library was to move, once again, years later, the building on Twelfth Street, between McGee and Oak, continues to serve as headquarters for the Kansas City, Missouri, School District. It was not until 1988 that the library was separated from the district's control. It then became a "public" library in every sense of the word. A few months later, the Library District's first board was organized.

THE KANSAS CITY "CENTRAL" PUBLIC LIBRARY AT TENTH STREET AND MAIN STREET

By the 1990s, it became clear that a more adequate library building was needed. Plans were initiated to move the library into the former home of the First National Bank, at 14 West Tenth Street. Like its earlier home at Ninth Street and Locust Street, it is an architecturally significant structure. The current facility features state-of-the-art technology, improved and increased services, meeting rooms, and a screening room. It also houses a jewel of a research center: the Missouri Valley Room, where the Missouri Valley Special Collections are located. This collection boasts a wealth of information for researchers and historians alike. Needless to say, it includes Carrie Westlake Whitney's three volumes of *Kansas City, Missouri: Its History and Its People 1808-1908.*

The Kansas City Public Library, 14 West Tenth Street, 2016

Harry S. Truman at age thirty-four
129th Field Artillery, World War I
France, 1918
Source: The Harry S. Truman Library & Museum

HARRY TRUMAN

ON A PERSONAL NOTE

EARLY MILITARY SERVICE

There were signs of Harry Truman's sense of patriotic duty long before he became Commander-in-Chief in 1945. He sacrificed much to enlist in the army during World War I. As a farmer he could have easily skipped active military duty. But his conscience would not allow him to shrink from his responsibility. So, in 1917, he left his mother and sister to run the farm and he put off his marriage to Bess Wallace. He enlisted in Battery D, and after eight months of training his artillery unit was sent to France and attached to the 35th Division. It was with Battery D, during the campaigns of 1918 in Brittany, where he excelled as its commanding officer. It was here that he was first called "Captain Harry" by his comrades, who respected him for his leadership and unflinching work ethic.

Truman's early military service shaped his destiny. It prepared him for the many challenges that he was to face in the years ahead—in his personal, business and political relationships. There was also that experience gained in World War I that he would call on during his days as president during the closing months of the next world war and the Korean conflict that followed.

Left: Sewing kit, extra lens for his glasses, and a letter home to Bess
Right: First Lt. Harry S. Truman, World War I
Battery D, 129th Field Artillery, June 1917
Source: The Harry S. Truman Library & Museum

WHILE JACKSON COUNTY PRESIDING JUDGE

"THE PICKWICK PAPERS"

There is an enlightening glimpse into the personal life and thoughts during his tenure as presiding judge of Jackson County. They can be found in "The Pickwick Papers" at the Harry S. Truman Library & Museum. They are summarized on the library's website: "Between 1930 and 1934, Truman occasionally took refuge at the Pickwick Hotel in downtown Kansas City. He had become increasingly tense, prone to headaches and insomnia, and the Pickwick was a place where he could think and work uninterrupted. During his stays, Truman became introspective, pouring out his thoughts about Jackson County politics and personalities on page after page of hotel stationery. He described the corruption he had witnessed and the ethical dilemmas he faced. His 'Pickwick Papers' provide remarkable insight into the difficulties a future President struggled with early in his political career."

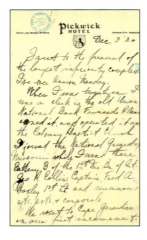  

Left: An entry in Harry Truman's journal, written at the Pickwick Hotel on December 3, 1930
Source: The Harry S. Truman Library & Museum
Center: Coffee cup and saucer from the Pickwick Hotel
Source: The Tom Taylor Collection
Right: Postcard of the Pickwick Hotel and Bus Terminal
Source: The Steve Noll Collection

FRIENDSHIPS

The day after the funeral of President Franklin D. Roosevelt, President Truman delivered his first address to a joint session of Congress. In the address he honored the memory of President Roosevelt and he made a pact with all Americans that he would fight for the defeat of Nazi Germany and Japan, while promising to support the ideals of justice, peace, and liberty. A few words from his address included:

It is with a heavy heart that I stand before you, my friends and colleagues, in the Congress of the United States. Only yesterday we laid to rest the mortal remains of our beloved President, Franklin Delano Roosevelt. At a time like this, words are inadequate. The most eloquent tribute would be a reverent silence.

Tragic fate has thrust upon us grave responsibilities. We must carry on. Our departed leader never looked backward. He looked forward and moved forward. That is what he would want us to do. That is what America will do.

Today, the entire world is looking to America for enlightened leadership to peace and progress. Such a leadership requires vision, courage and tolerance. It can be provided only by a united nation deeply devoted to the highest ideals.

I want in turn to assure my fellow Americans and all of those who love peace and liberty throughout the world that I will support and defend those ideals with all my strength and all my heart. That is my duty and I shall not shirk it.

Like most Americans, Truman's friend William O. Norman from Kansas City tuned his radio for the broadcast. Norman was a business associate of Harry Truman and a fellow Shriner and Mason, and at the time of Truman's ascent to the presidency he was president of the City Bond & Mortgage Co. Norman was so taken with the moment and the new president's humble words that he immediately sent off a letter of support. He wrote:

April 16, 1945

My Dear Mr. President:

I am very proud of you.

You made a great speech today. The American people could not help but love you.

I know you will be a great President. You shall always have my prayers and best wishes. If you think I could be of help to you — all you need to do is just let me know.

Your true friend, W. O. Norman

The President promptly responded:

April 21, 1945

My Dear Billy:

Your letter means a great deal to me. Such loyal friendship is a tremendous help and it will sustain me to know that I shall have your prayers and good wishes in the days ahead.

Very sincerely yours,

Harry Truman

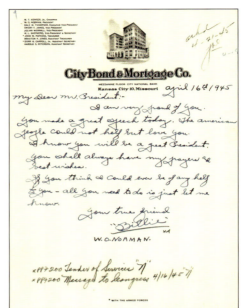

Left: W. O. Norman
Source: The Kansas City Museum
Right: April 16, 1945, letter from W. O. Norman to President Harry S. Truman
Source: The Harry S. Truman Library & Museum

Left: April 21, 1945, letter from President Harry S. Truman to W. O. Norman
Source: The Bill and Jeri Murphy Collection
Right: President Harry S. Truman
Source: The Harry S. Truman Library & Museum

Truman was both a Shriner and a Thirty-third Degree Mason. Through his involvement with these organizations, he made many lasting friendships. Norman was among them.

Left: Souvenir Shriners' hat, presented to President Truman
Right: Ring presented to President Truman when he became a Thirty-third Degree Mason
Source, both: The Harry S. Truman Library & Museum

THE NATIONAL PASTIME

It can be argued that of the two, Truman's wife Bess was the bigger fan of baseball. As president, however, the position did have its perks when it came to the national pastime. For example, he was treated to a season pass in 1951 (the 50th anniversary of the American League), to any stadium in the country. The pass was good for "Harry S. Truman and Party." Bess had one of her own.

Left: Baseball cap, Kansas City Blues (American Association), 1953
Right: Baseball cap, Kansas City Athletics, 1955
Source: The Harry S. Truman Library & Museum

Top left: 1951 American League pass, Harry S. Truman and Party
Top right: Lowell's Trophy, for "Highest Baseball I.Q."
Awarded to President Truman in 1949
Bottom left: Official American League Baseball, autographed by
Charles O. Finley, owner of the Kansas City Athletics
Bottom right: 1957 American League pass, Bess Wallace Truman and Party
Source: The Harry S. Truman Library & Museum

FAMILY

Harry S. Truman: His Life and Times exhibit at The Harry S. Truman Library & Museum

Left: Family records inscribed in the Truman Family Bible
Right: *The Corner White House*, by Matthew Monks
Source, left: Bruce Mathews photos for The Harry S. Truman Library & Museum
Source: The Gloria Dobbs and Courtney Sloan Collection

Left: Bruce Mathews' photo of statue of President Truman, and his grandson
Clifton Truman Daniel, holding a photo of his third-great-grandmother, Nancy Tyler Holmes
Right: Margaret Truman returning to Kansas City for the wedding of her friend
Mary "Shawsie" Shaw to Coleman Branton
Source: The Harry S. Truman Library & Museum

More than fifty of Truman's ancestors and relatives are buried in Kansas City's historic Elmwood Cemetery. While working on the book *Elmwood Cemetery: Stories of Kansas City*, I had the honor of photographing the former president's grandson, Clifton Truman Daniel (one of Margaret's sons), holding a photo of his third-great-grandmother, Nancy (Tyler) Holmes, who is buried in Elmwood.

In the photo on the right (above), Margaret Truman is seen after her arrival at Kansas City's Municipal Airport. She had returned from Washington, DC, to serve as a bridesmaid at the wedding of her lifelong friend, Mary Shaw ("Shawsie") to Coleman Branton, on April 12, 1947.

Pedal car given to Margaret Truman by her parents, Christmas 1926
Source: The Harry S. Truman Library & Museum

As told by Clay Bauske, curator at the The Harry S. Truman Library & Museum: "This pedal car was under the Truman's Christmas tree in 1926. Designed to look like a Packard, it has a wooden frame supporting an iron body, axles, wheels and steering wheel. Because her father had frequently taken her on highway inspection tours, Margaret described herself as 'road conscious' and happy to help her friends 'engineer complicated networks of roads and highways in the newest designs,' all in her own backyard. The Truman Christmas tree of that year shows both the pedal car and Margaret's baby carriage, which now offered transportation for her many dolls.

Baby carriage and tricycle belonging to Harry and Bess Truman's daughter, Margaret
Source, all: The Harry S. Truman Library & Museum

Shown here at the age of four, Margaret loved this Pioneer tricycle made by Gendron Wheel Company of Toledo, Ohio, who advertised that "outdoor play makes happy, healthy children." Most of Margaret's friends also had "wheels" and "the tricycle and scooter traffic in the driveway was intense." Margaret regularly was forgiven by Grandmother Wallace for "tearing around and around the house on my tricycle knocking the patina off the antiques."

President Truman's "Iron Curtain Speech" pocket watch
Source: The Harry S. Truman Library & Museum

This gold pocket watch was a gift to Harry Truman from Westminster College (Fulton, Missouri) on the occasion of English Prime Minister Winston Churchill's "Iron Curtain Speech" there, by invitation of President Truman, on March 5, 1946. The back of the watch is engraved: "To Harry S. Truman / President of the United States / March 5, 1946 / from the faculty and students."

Bess Truman's bridge club
Bess Truman: fourth from right
Source: The Jim Noel Collection

Her bridge club, comprising her friends from Independence, played an important role in the social life of Bess Wallace Truman. In this photo she is surrounded by bridge club members: Mary G. Shaw, Linda King, Natalie Ott Wallace, Helena F. Crow, Meg Barkley Noel, Edna Hutchinson, Adelaide Twyman, Thelma Pallette, Lucy Peters, and Mary Wallace. Bess Truman is fourth from the right.

REMEMBERED

**Secretary of State Gen. Colin Powell,
at the gravesite of President and Mrs. Truman
Fiftieth anniversary of President Truman's executive order
desegregating the Armed Forces
1998**
Source: Bruce Mathews photo for The Harry S. Truman Library & Museum

Author's note: In 1998, I had the honor of photographing Gen. Powell in a private moment, as he paid tribute to the former Commander-in-Chief at the Truman Library. Powell had come to Independence to speak on the fiftieth anniversary of Truman's landmark executive order desegregating the Armed Forces. That presidential decree paved the way for Powell's rise to the position of chairman of the joint chiefs of staff, and ultimately to his role as secretary of state.

So, as I empty the drawer of this desk, and Mrs. Truman and I leave the White House,
we have no regret. We feel we have done our best in the public service.
I hope and believe we have contributed to the welfare of this Nation
and to the peace of the world.

Harry S. Truman
From the Farewell Address to the American People
January 15, 1953
Source: The Harry S. Truman Library & Museum

THE BUCK STOPS HERE!
President Harry S. Truman
Source: The John Dillingham Collection

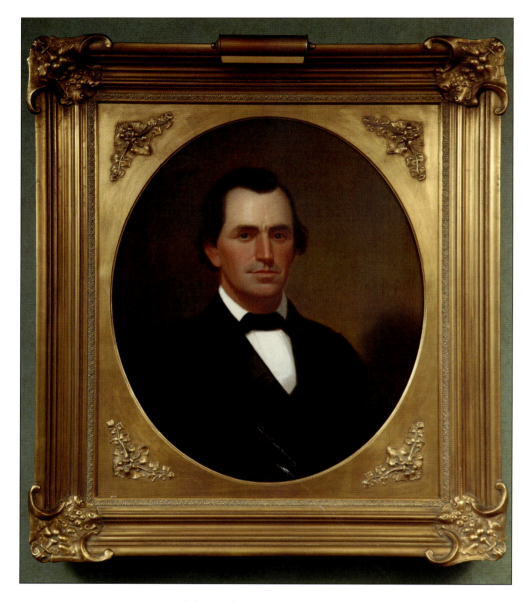

George Caleb Bingham portrait of John B. Wornall
Source: The John B. Wornall IV Collection

To Eliza…. "My circumstances in life make it expedient for me to seek one to share with me its ills and partake of life of its joys, and could I influence thee dear girl to occupy that position, if I could but hope, the sorrows of this life to be but light and few…."
Yours devotedly,
John B. Wornall

THE PROPOSAL

THE MARRIAGE OF JOHN B. WORNALL AND ELIZA JOHNSON

George Caleb Bingham portrait of Eliza
Source: The Charlotte and Stephen Kirk Collection

Mr. Wornall…after due consideration
I am prepared to answer you in the affirmative.
Eliza

John Bristow Wornall Sr. and Eliza Shalcross Johnson were married September 20, 1854. He was thirty-one and she was eighteen. John was the son of Richard and Judith Ann (Glover) Wornall, of Kentucky. Eliza was the daughter of the founder of the Shawnee Methodist Mission, the Rev. Thomas Johnson and his wife, Sarah (Davis).

John Wornall's proposal of marriage to Eliza Johnson
Source: The Charlotte and Stephen Kirk Collection

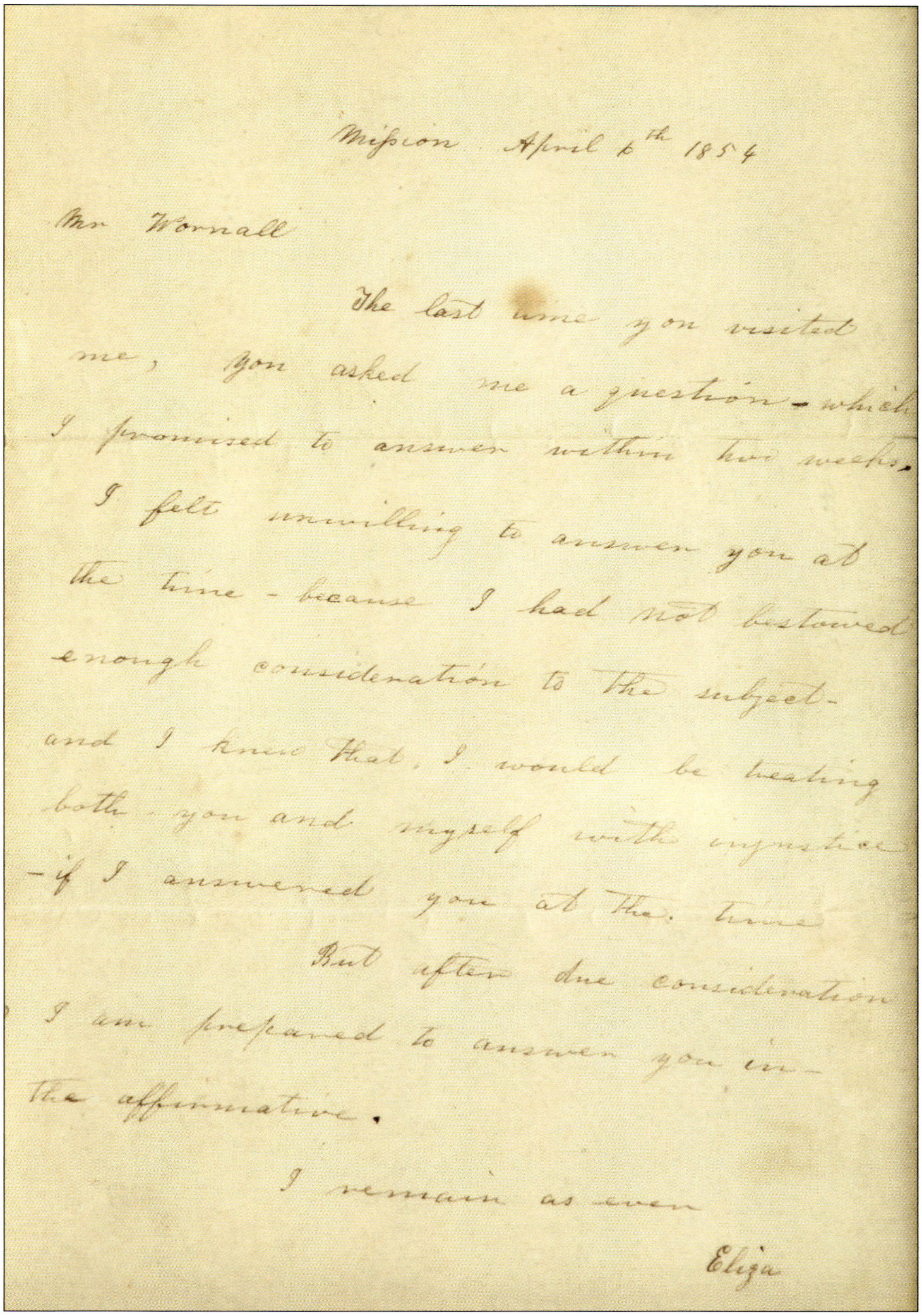

Mission April 6th 1854

Mr Wornall

The last time you visited
me, You asked me a question - which
I promised to answer within two weeks.
I felt unwilling to answer you at
the time - because I had not bestowed
enough consideration to the subject.
and I knew that, I would be treating
both you and myself with injustice
- if I answered you at the time
But after due consideration
I am prepared to answer you in -
the affirmative.

I remain as ever

Eliza

Eliza's response to the proposal of marriage
Source: The Charlotte and Stephen Kirk Collection

Left: Early portraits of John and Eliza Wornall, circa 1854
Right: One of Eliza's linen handkerchiefs
Source: The Charlotte and Stephen Kirk Collection

Left: John B. Wornall's rocking chair on display in the Wornall House Museum
Source: The Wornall House Museum Collection
Right: The grandfather clock brought by the Wornall family from Kentucky
Source: The John B. Wornall IV Collection

Wornall Family Reunion – 2003
Source: The Charlotte and Stephen Kirk Collection

John B. Wornall stands among the most notable of the early pioneers of Westport and Kansas City. While his wealth resulted from his knowledge and determination, it was also made possible by the use of hired labor and slaves. A successful farmer, Wornall also achieved prominence in the field of real estate. The city father helped to better farming methods in the region by founding the Jackson County Agricultural and Mechanical Association, which he also served as president. He helped to found the First National Bank of Kansas City, and he donated the land upon which the Calvary Baptist Church was built. He served as a trustee and benefactor of William Jewell College in nearby Liberty, Missouri. Wornall's role as a civic leader led him to serve in the Missouri State Senate. Located on what is now Wornall Road, his stately Greek Revival home served both sides as a field hospital during the Battle of Westport.

Wornall married Matilda Polk[e] in 1850. She died the following year, leaving no children. He then wed Eliza, by whom he fathered five children: Francis Clay, Fannie, Sallie, Edna, and Thomas Johnson. After Eliza's death in 1865, Wornall married Roma Johnson. The couple had two sons, John Bristow Jr. and Charles Hardin Wornall.

As with many of the early Kansas City and Westport families their legacies can best be measured by the contributions many of their heirs have made for the betterment of the community.

And now the circle is complete.
We come together as family to share a wonderful meal
and make new memories,
to be passed along by the next generation
with lots of love and butter.

– Gayle and Bruce - 11/26/99

THE KRIGEL FAMILY HISTORY TABLE

by Gayle Krigel

Through forty years of marriage, each piece of art that Bruce and I have acquired has its own unique history. The story of each item in our collection might include a place that we were traveling or a philanthropic event where it was displayed. We love each of these pieces because of the memories they evoke. Perhaps our favorite acquisition is Bruce's Great-Aunt Hélène's game table.

Great-Aunt Hélène and her husband, Great-Uncle Eli, lived in Oklahoma City. He was the brother of Bruce's grandfather, an Indiana-born, Michigan-educated lawyer, who fell in love with Grandma Nellie. She was a native of Oklahoma City, born to the Herskowitz family, prominent businessmen and real estate developers. In fact, they built the first "skyscraper" in Oklahoma City's downtown, the five-story Herskowitz Building.

The game table with two leaves was given to Bruce's mother, Marjorie, and was used for extra dinner seating when needed. It was an ugly blond wood with black marble inserts and had matching chairs with black leather upholstery. It was not remarkable in any way except that it had "good bones" and some interesting stories of those who had shared meals around it.

To start, there was Great-Aunt Hélène, whose red lipstick flowed freely outside her lip-lines and who never had any children of her own. Not understanding the culinary likes and dislikes of young people, she served raw oysters and smoked clams to Bruce and his sister. It was this tidbit of information that prompted us to have the table frame whimsically distressed in yellow with touches of every other color imaginable and to write a snippet about past and current diners.

Grandma Marge Krigel was a volunteer extraordinaire, as well as a travel agent. Her favorite ingredient was Lawry's Salt. Grandpa Jack went to Harvard Law School. Although he loved good food and was always complimentary when invited to dine at our home, he possessed absolutely zero cooking skills. Jeff, our youngest, loved to hear the stories behind our inherited silver and china, while he helped set the table for family holiday gatherings. Eliyahu, our oldest, is a Jewish educator and keeps kosher. At one time he was also a vegetarian, so Jeff dubbed him a "koshertarian." Emily, our middle child, has always been a peacemaker, in school, and with friends and family--it's just her sweet disposition and her calling in life. Her favorite food is mac and cheese. All of these stories are chronicled, handwritten around the table's apron.

Bruce and I love to entertain and we do it often. We worked together in our wholesale distribution business, and our house has always been a gathering spot for family and friends. Our table shares our "secret" ingredient (just add butter) and tales of each family member's demeanor, favorite food or culinary expertise. It's a work of art and a history of the Krigels, creatively documented for generations to come.

Although our children are all minimalists in a way, each has expressed an interest in having our family-history table in his/her own home, when we're "done" with it! I've often thought about starting a business to help other families create a masterpiece of art history for future generations.

**Sally Kaney in the wedding dress from her 1942 marriage
to George Washington Tourtellot III**
Source: The Kansas City Museum Collection

Sally Kaney married George W. Tourtellot III on June 6, 1942, during World War II. Her wedding dress featured handmade lace from Belgium, brought back from a trip taken by George's grandmother. The gown was made for and first worn by Sally's mother-in-law, Margaret "Madge" Topping, when she became the bride of George Washington Tourtellot Jr., on June 10, 1910. Next in line was Margaret E. "Peggy" Tourtellot, the sister of Sally's husband, when she wed David Oliver Smart III. The dress was last worn by Sally. It has received a permanent home in the wedding dress collection of the Kansas City Museum.

SALLY, FAMILY, AND FRIENDS

At various times in her life, Sally Lee Kaney Tourtellot Ruddy has been a model, artist, sculptor, photographer, poet, producer, writer, activist, rancher, and world traveler. She is also an avid collector of treasures, friends, and stories. Sally Ruddy is ninety-four years young. She vividly recalls the fond and bittersweet memories collected throughout her life's journey.

Sally was born shortly after the end of World War I, the daughter of Cliff and Marguerite "Polly" Kaney. At the beginning of World War II, she married George W. Tourtellot III. Tragically, her husband died far too early, as the result of his top-secret experiments with radar during wartime. The long-term exposure to cancer-causing elements used in the experiments was responsible for his death on August 17, 1964, at the age of forty-nine. Ten years later Sally would marry the widower John Ruddy, vice-president with the J. C. Nichols Co. John had four children by his first marriage to add to Sally's three by hers. He was always a great comfort and guiding influence for all seven children. He passed away in 1991.

Left: Sally and George on their wedding day, June 6, 1942
Right: George, while stationed in the Aleutian Islands during World War II
Source: The Sally Ruddy Collection

Sally grew up in the saddle, riding at her father's side in the stockyards of Kansas City. Displaying her wide range of talents at an early age, she worked for a time as a photographer for the J.C. Nichols Company. She created Nichols's now-iconic portrait, taken for his biography, titled *The J.C. Nichols Chronicle: The Authorized Story of the Man, His Company and His Legacy.* Over the years, Sally has amassed an amazing collection of treasures. To say the collection is eclectic would be an understatement. Containing many items of her own creation, it spans decades of Kansas City history and represents a colorful look at unique slices of Americana. But nothing else would be expected from such a unique treasure in her own right.

> *"The fortunate ones are those who really know what they want to do*
> *with their life. If you can do what you've always wanted to,*
> *you'll be happy and fulfilled. I hooked my wagon to a star*
> *a long time ago, and it's been a tremendous ride."*
> —Philippe de Rosier, 1918-1991

 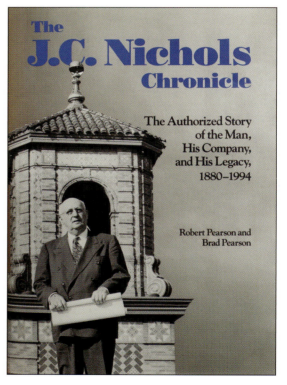

Left: Sally Tourtellot at the time she photographed J.C. Nichols
Right: *The J.C. Nichols Chronicle* book cover
Source, both: The Sally Ruddy Collection

George Tourtellot had operated Miracle Pictures, a commercial photography business, before World War II. His clever slogan was "If It's Good, It's a Miracle." Among his clients was the J.C. Nichols Company, developers of the renowned Country Club Plaza, as well as numerous fine residential neighborhoods. When her husband was stationed overseas, Sally took over the photography business. She did such a masterful job that Nichols would always declare her portrait of him to be his all-time favorite.

SALLY'S FATHER, CLIFF KANEY

Left: Portrait of Cliff Kaney, Sally's father
painted by artist Dwight Roberts
Right: Key to the City presented by Mayor H. Roe Bartle to Cliff Kaney
Source: The Sally Ruddy Collection

Sally's father, Cliff Kaney (or "Cliffy," as she called him), was president of the Swift and Henry Live Stock Commission Company. The firm was one of the largest commission businesses in the country. Kaney was intimately involved in the business and civic circles of Kansas City. He served as chairman of the Greater Kansas City Chamber of Commerce, and he was president of the Kansas City Livestock Exchange for seven years. Kaney's portrait is the work of noted artist Dwight Roberts; it hangs on the wall of Sally's dining room. Sally's artistic talents were enhanced by attending classes given by Roberts. He later relocated to Santa Fe, New Mexico, where he opened the Kachina Gallery.

Hanging from the frame is the "Key to the City," presented to Kaney by Mayor H. Roe Bartle in recognition of the civic leader's lifelong commitment to Kansas City. Kaney and his friend Jay Dillingham have been the only two presidents of the Livestock Exchange to have also presided over the Greater Kansas City Chamber of Commerce. Both men have received the esteemed key.

Jay Dillingham on the left and Cliff Kaney on the right at the Kansas City Stockyards
Source: The John Dillingham Collection

75th Anniversary pin and the 1963 American Royal, First Vice-President pin worn by Cliff Kaney
Source, both: The Sally Ruddy Collection

Kaney was a business associate and personal friend of Bill Deramus, president of Kansas City Southern Railway. After the passenger train the *Southern Belle* made its maiden voyage to New Orleans, Deramus had the bell from the engine removed. He then presented it as a gift to Kaney. The bell occupies a special place on Sally's farm. In a close personal connection to Kansas City Southern, Sally became a close friend of Sarah and Landon Rowland. Rowland rose to prominence with Kansas City Southern; Kansas City lost a civic giant when he passed away in 2016. Sally is the godmother to Sarah and Landon's son Joshua.

Left: Engine bell from the maiden voyage of the *Southern Belle* passenger train
Source: The Sally Ruddy Collection
Right: Advertisement for passenger travel on the *Southern Belle*
Source: Missouri Valley Special Collections, Kansas City Public Library

WHAT'S IN A NAME?

It is often interesting to learn the derivation of given names passed down from generation to generation within a family. In certain cases, the stories are downright hilarious. Consider the name George Washington Tourtellot. It turns out that George Washington Tourtellot Sr. was not even born with the name.

The story goes that the patriarch was the first-born son of Paris and Mary Ann (Stephens) Tourtellot. He arrived on the scene in 1846, with the given name of Dallas. As a boy, Dallas had a young black playmate named George Washington Jackson. The boys especially enjoyed exploring the nearby woods together. On one occasion, when they met at a favorite creek, Dallas was sporting a brand-new pair of bright red boots. Young George Washington Jackson coveted the boots, and it turned out that Dallas preferred his friend's name to his own. A deal was struck: the youngsters swapped names for boots.

When young Tourtellot returned home minus his new boots, he explained to his parents that he had traded the boots for a new name. His astonished mother and father were so taken with the story that they had their son's name officially changed to George Washington Tourtellot! The year was 1855, six years before the outbreak of the Civil War.

This lad would grow up making quite a name for himself, serving as general superintendent for Armour & Company, one of the largest meat-packing operations in the country. Each generation of descendants have built upon the family name in their own way. It is an unlikely saga begun by a boy who traded a pair of shiny red boots for his name.

**Left: Pocket watch worn by George W. Tourtellot Sr.,
while serving as general superintendent for Armour & Co.**
Source: The Sally Ruddy Collection
Right: Postcard view of the Armour & Co. plant – Kansas City
Source: The Tom Taylor Collection

George Tourtellot Jr., the father of Sally's husband George III, had a successful career in real estate, retiring from the J.C. Nichols Company after fifty-four years with the company. At the time of his retirement, Miller Nichols, the son of the company's founder, penned a "Special Bulletin to All Personnel." Dated July 1, 1963, it highlighted Tourtellot's many achievements. One of them was described this way: "One of his interesting assignments was the assembling of the land which today comprises the Country Club Plaza. This project was not easy, and it required several years before it was completed. Prior to our ownership, the Plaza site had been sold off in small 40 foot lots, and in the intervening years the owners had scattered from New York to San Francisco, and one was in India. Some had died, and it was necessary to locate the heirs. Needless to say, it was an interesting and time-consuming project, but otherwise there would not have been a Country Club Plaza."

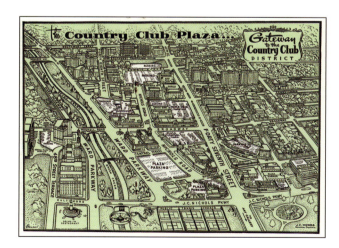

Overview of the Country Club Plaza from an early Plaza Directory
Source: The Dick Rees Collection

THE LYRIC OPERA

Sally served on the board of the Kansas City Lyric Opera for many years. In 1968, she created ceramic figures to decorate the tables for the Lyric Ball held in Union Station. The clever creations depicted characters appearing in the four perfomances of the Lyric Opera that year. The statue on the left was taken from *Tales of Hoffman*. The central characters, Rudolfo and Mimi, were featured in *La Bohème*. The figure on the right appeared in Shakespeare's comedy *The Taming of the Shrew*. Sally served as chair of the Lyric Ball in 1972, when the event was held at Crown Center.

**Sally and her ceramic figures, created for
the 1968 Lyric Opera Ball held at Union Station**
Source: The Sally Ruddy Collection

THE CAMELLOT ACADEMY

In 1966, renowned musical director Mel Bishop became inspired by a young student named Gina Bikales, as she related her experiences during four years at summer camp at the University of Kansas. The music and

**A scene from *The Pirates of Penzance*, performed in 1967 by students of the Camellot Academy
at Unity Village. Seen on the right is a young cast member, Marshall Watson, who went on to
perform on TV and Broadway. He is now enjoying a highly successful career in interior design,
operating Marshall Watson Interiors in New York City.**
Source: The Sally Ruddy Collection.

art camps held there left a lasting imprint upon her life. Bishop hoped to create a similar environment in Kansas City. Sally Ruddy was among those involved in the formation of the institution that became the Camellot Academy. Sally wisely approached her father, Cliff Kaney, who responded: "If Mel Bishop would like to start a summer camp for young people, I will help to finance it, if you will do the work." Of Mel Bishop, director of music at Southwest High School, as well as the Barstow, Pembroke, and Sunset Hill schools, Kaney remarked: "Mel has such a special talent." The following summer, Camellot Academy opened its doors at Unity Village in Lee's Summit. The school included a faculty of ten and an enrollment of eighty high school students.

Camellot Academy is the oldest performing and fine arts camp in Kansas City, with an emphasis upon Broadway Theater. It offers classes in art, dance, drama, and vocal music. Today, the camp is located at Rockhurst High School, where it offers performance opportunities for boys and girls between the ages of five and fourteen.

PUPPETS

Sally Ruddy has been deeply involved in the arts her entire life. Making puppets and staging productions for the Kansas City Toy and Miniature Museum has been among her many creative endeavors. She and her dear friend Sarah Rowland took their shows on the road, delighting crowds of children and adults throughout the Kansas City metropolitan area. The photos featured here illustrate only a few of the hundreds of puppets, sets, and promotional artwork Sally has crafted. Among her creations is a self-portrait puppet, with paintbrush in hand; it illustrates the "whatever-it-takes" attitude Sally has always personified, ensuring that no detail is left untouched. Also shown is a model of the twelve-by-twelve-foot stage Sally's friend Philippe de Rosier designed for her production of *Punch and Judy*.

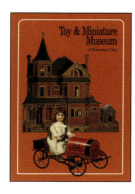  

Left and center: 1992 Kansas Toy and Miniature Museum booklet
featuring puppet stage designed for Sally by G. Philippe de Rosier
Right: Model created by Philippe de Rosier
Source: The Sally Ruddy Collection

Puppets and artwork created by Sally Ruddy for her many puppet shows
Source, all: The Sally Ruddy Collection

The attractive brass containers that hold Sally's sculpting tools represent an excellent example of repurposing while keeping history alive. Originally, they rested on the floor of the main waiting room in Kansas City's Union Station, where they functioned as stylish hardware on the legs of benches used by the thousands of travelers who waited to board their trains. Sally purchased two of the benches at an auction held at the station many years ago. The repurposed tool holders serve as poignant reminders of the events the benches have witnessed over the years.

**Sculpting tool holders repurposed from benches formerly located
in the North Waiting Room of Union Station, Kansas City**
Source: The Sally Ruddy Collection

AN ARTIST NEVER STOPS CREATING

In 2002, at the age of eighty, Sally was invited to design one of the White House Christmas Tree ornaments for President George W. Bush and First Lady Laura Bush. Two artists from each state were selected to create the series, with instructions that the decorations should feature historic homes. Conforming to strict guidelines offered from the White House with respect to size and weight, Sally fashioned an ornament dedicated to former president Harry S. Truman. Titled "The Man for All Seasons," it depicts President Truman in front of his Independence home during each season of the year. The original piece resides in the archives of the White House Historical Society. Sally keeps this replica on display in her studio in Lee's Summit, Missouri.

**Replica of the White House Christmas Tree ornament
created by Sally Ruddy in 2002**
Source: The Sally Ruddy Collection

KINDRED SPIRITS

While working on *Windows of Kansas City: As Art, History and Inspiration*, I had the privilege of becoming acquainted with the wonderfully talented artist Philomene Bennett. Philomene had designed stained-glass windows for the St. Charles Borromeo Parish Church, which I included in the book. When we first met, I knew instantly that she and Sally were "kindred spirits." The two creative souls simply had to meet. After working up the courage, I asked Philomene if I could pick her up, take her to Sally's home, and introduce the two of them. They hit it off spectacularly. Fortunately, I took my camera along and took a photo of the two ladies, swinging on a bench in Sally's home, surrounded by her artwork. As it happened, during the Vietnam War era, Sally had taken an art class instructed by Philomene. They had not met since. What a memorable reunion it turned out to be.

Philomene Bennett on the left and Sally Ruddy on the right
March 13, 2014

THE ONE CONSTANT

The one constant throughout Sally's life has been her special friendship with David Douglas Duncan, who grew up in Kansas City, Missouri, two houses down from the Kaneys on West Fifty-seventh Street. Duncan became one of the world's most renowned war photographers, capturing harrowing combat scenes during World War II, the Korean Conflict, and the Vietnam War. It was Duncan who introduced Sally to his friend, George Tourtellot. After the couple married, they shared many happy occasions with Duncan and his wife.

At the time of this writing, David, now living in France, has celebrated his one-hundredth birthday. He has always taken great pride in lifelong good health. While his age does not permit him to fly to the United States any-more, he and Sally enjoy frequent telephone conversations.

An endearing entry appears in Sally's personal journal. It concerns her first en-counter with Duncan, who is seven years her senior. She was in grade school when the Kaneys moved into the neighborhood. Sally shares Duncan's recol-lections of that moment: "One fall day, before school started, I was in our back yard with a bunch of guys. We were talking about school and how we wished summer vacation would last forever. A couple of the boys were holding a big black snake. Then all at once there was this girl walking into my my yard from two doors away. That corner house had been sold to new owners. No one in the neighborhood knew much about them. But I guessed this girl came from the family in that house. The two boys holding the black snake saw the girl the same time I saw her. They advanced toward her thrusting the snake at her in a threatening way. I stepped between the boys with the snake and the girl. Facing the boys I said, 'You will not tease her.' She looked at me with big eyes in her small thin face. It wasn't the look of someone frightened — it was as though she was happy that I felt she needed protecting. Then just before she turned to back to her yard, she reached back to pat the snake the boys were holding. I thought at that moment I would never forget her. I never did."

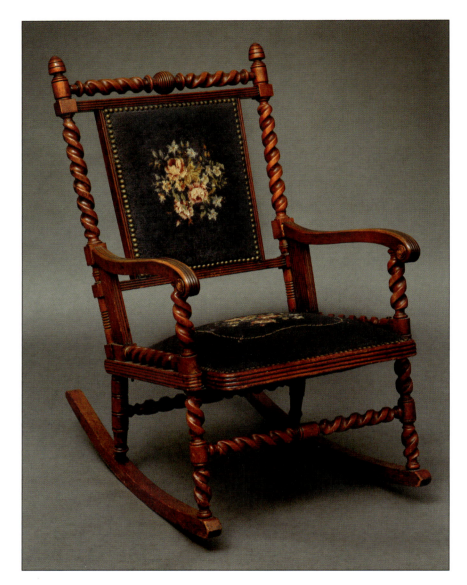

**The Kearney family rocking chair used by Hattie Drisdom Kearney
to rock generations of Kearney and Wornall children**
Source: Rowland Nofsinger

The story of Hattie Drisdom Kearney reflects the complex
societal conditions before, during and after the Civil War.
It is a story of slavery, of utter disregard of human dignity.
It is also a story of compassion for the least among us.

*– Kansas City's Historic Union Cemetery:
Lessons for the Future, from the Garden of Time*

HATTIE'S ROCKING CHAIR

Charles Kearney is among those early pioneers of Kansas City whose role in shaping the destiny of our community is easily overlooked. The passage of time, however, cannot diminish his character and the mark he left. Kearney was a staunch Union supporter in a town heavily influenced by Southern views on slavery. He was a successful businessman and civic leader, respected by everyone who knew him. He was a freighter on the Santa Fe Trail, and he operated a dry goods store. He was also a bond trader. After his marriage to Josephine Harris, he operated the Harris House Hotel at the corner of Westport Road and Pennsylvania Avenue.

He left his mark on the landscape of Kansas City by playing a significant role in the building of the town's first bridge across the Missouri River. The Kansas City Bridge, known today as the Hannibal Bridge, secured the foundation for the city's growth. Opened in 1869, it allowed Texas cattle to be brought to the region aboard the Hannibal & St. Joseph Railway. It also helped protect Kansas City's economy from the ruinous effects of the Civil War.

But the true legacy of a man cannot be measured in terms of financial achievement or civic accomplishment: his real worth is evidenced in the strength of his character. Kearney will be remembered as a man who made the world a better place by virtue of his honor and integrity.

Col. Charles Esmonde Kearney
Source: The Kansas City Museum

The only known photo of Hattie Drisdom Kearney,
standing alone outside of the Harris-Kearney House, circa 1920
Source: The Westport Historical Society

The story begins in 1844, when Harriet "Hattie" Drisdom was born to slave parents in Westport, Missouri. Eleven years later, the young girl found herself on the slave auction block in her hometown, where she was sold for $1,300. This tragic event might have ended Hattie's potential for future success. But however unlikely it was, the auction marked the beginning of a long and meaningful life for young Hattie.

On that fateful day in 1855, one of the bidders determined to take Hattie home as a possession, and he raised the stakes. He was a cruel master, known for hiring out his slaves and literally working them to death. During the course of the bidding, Hattie spotted the kind face of the colonel. She begged him to enter the bidding, and he complied. The auction for Hattie concluded with Kearney as the highest bidder. He had spent $1,300 for the sole purpose of giving Hattie her freedom.

Hattie's situation appeared to be a bleak one, nevertheless. What were the chances of an eleven-year-old mulatto child surviving by herself during those times? But Kearney and his wife, Josephine, allowed Hattie to spend two years in their household. After that time, the colonel granted the girl her freedom while offering her a position as nurse and companion to the Kearneys' four children. Hattie Drisdom became a beloved member of the Kearney family, taking care of their three sons and only daughter. The relationship was one of mutual love and respect, and Hattie accepted no wages for her service.

Hattie's rocking chair became a symbol of that loving bond. In her special chair, she would comfort several generations of Kearneys. After the death of the colonel and his wife, Hattie moved into the home of their daughter Julia, who had married Frank Wornall.

Col. Kearney's funeral was held at Union Cemetery on January 5, 1898. Thousands of Kansas Citians joined the family in the graveside tribute.

Mrs. Frank Wornall (Julia Kearney)
Source: The Kansas City Museum

In a cruel twist of fate, pickpockets were at work in the crowd, and Hattie became one of the victims. She was robbed of her entire life savings of $400, as she stood weeping at the graveside of the man who had effectively saved her life, some forty-three years earlier.

Hattie lived for thirty years after the death of her benefactor. She took the Kearney family name, which is inscribed on her tombstone in the family's lot in Union Cemetery. She was the first person of color to be interred in the "white" section of that burial ground. The headline in the Kansas City Journal on the day after Hattie's funeral read: "White Folks Bow at Bier of Old Hattie."

Julia (Kearney) Wornall summed up the feelings of the entire family this way: "We simply would not have the public look on Hattie as a servant. We've considered her more than a servant, an intimate friend. She was almost a member of the family and it pleased all of us to show her every consideration. But, aside from that, Hattie was the most faithful, unselfish friend and companion our children ever had. She 'mothered' all of the children; taught them how to play and took care of them even after they were grown men and women."

As for the rocking chair, by the beginning of the twenty-first century it had worked its way down to the family of Rowland Nofsinger. In 2015, the Nofsinger family donated that venerable piece of furniture to the Westport Historical Society for display in "Hattie's Room" at the Harris-Kearney House, which is the oldest residence in Kansas City. Located at 4000 Baltimore Avenue and listed on the National Register of Historic Places, the Harris-Kearney House is now a museum.

The gravestone of Hattie Drisdom Kearney, Union Cemetery, Kansas City, Missouri

Left to right: Maxine Gertrude Kubis (1911-1984), Bernice Lela Kubis (1916-1917),
Robert Glennon Kubis (1914-)
Source: Glenn and Nadine Kubis

THE KUBIS FAMILY PHOTOS

> *For the first time in his 100 years Glenn held in his hands the only photo he had ever seen of his baby sister.*
>
> – Bruce Mathews

There is a good reason why this feature occupies the last position in this collection of stories: it represents the summary of the remainder of the book. The Kubis family photos speak volumes in favor of the need for the preservation of family heirlooms to be passed along for the benefit of our children and our children's children. Alex Haley was speaking for all of us when he said, "There is a hunger, marrow-deep, to know who we are and where we have come from." The same holds true when considering the larger communities in which we live. How can we come together with any sense of community if we have nothing to look back on? For every building that is demolished, for every public record that is lost, for the identification of every person in a photo that goes unrecorded, a part of our legacy is lost.

In April of 2013, while working on a family history project, I had the honor of sitting down with Glenn and Nadine Kubis for an interview. At the

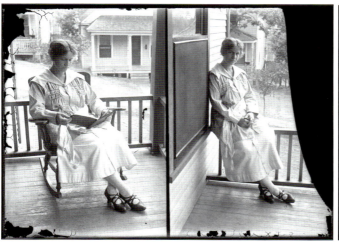

Left: Lela Edna (Spangler) Kubis (1889–1964)
Right: Lela Edna Kubis with her children Maxine Gertrude and Robert Glennon
on their front porch at 432 Donnelly St., Kansas City, Missouri
Source: Glenn and Nadine Kubis

time, Glenn was 99. Nadine was 93. Glenn was nearly blind, as a result of the German artillery flak he received during a nighttime parachute drop during World War II. We talked about Glenn's life growing up in Kansas City during the early part of the twentieth century, when he was a student at Northeast High School. We also spoke about his marriage to Nadine and his adventures in World War II.

About thirty minutes into our visit, Nadine left the room. When she returned, she was holding a package wrapped in old newspapers. She opened it. Inside were fifteen five-by-seven-inch glass plate negatives of family photos, all taken during the ten years between 1910 and 1920. The plates had been tucked away in a closet, and Glenn had never seen them as prints. Although they are slices of Americana, there was absolutely no identification associated with the plates. There was nothing to facilitate the placing of names to faces.

Glenn and Nadine observed that they would not be around much longer, and they asked me to take the plates for safekeeping. I had an even better idea: the photographs' new home would be in the archives of the Missouri Valley Special Collections at the Kansas City Public Library. Future historians and genealogists would treasure them immensely. However, before turning them over to the library, I offered to have the glass plates scanned as high-resolution digital files from which prints could easily be made. They would also be in a format that could be used for printing in a book such as this one.

The Kubis – Spangler family
Front row: Chester Claude Brooks, Robert Glennon Kubis, Maxine Gertrude Kubis
Middle row: Lillian Spangler Brooks Wampler, Gertrude Spangler Thomas, Mae Spangler
Back row: Roy S. Thomas, Robert E. Kubis, Lela Spangler Kubis, A. J. Spangler
Source: Glenn and Nadine Kubis

 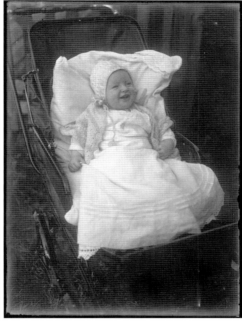 

Left to right: Maxine Gertrude, Bernice Lela and Robert Glennon Kubis
Source, all: Glenn and Nadine Kubis

The plates were scanned and prints were made. At that point, they truly became family treasures. I asked Glenn and Nadine to examine the prints and write down the names of anyone they recognized. I also asked them to identify any of the houses that looked familiar. They worked diligently, and at week's end, they had identified every person in every photo. Not only that, they had identified each home by address. Most of the people and the majority of homes are long gone; but we now have tangible evidence of the identities of the protagonists, their residences, and the appearances of both.

The most poignant story that results from these images can be found in a photograph taken in 1916. It shows Glenn at age two-and-a-half. He is sitting on the porch steps of the family home at 432 Donnelly Street in Kansas City, Missouri. With him is his five-year-old sister, Maxine Gertrude, and his one-year-old sister, Bernice Lela. In a sad twist of fate, Bernice died of diphtheria two years after her birth. Having never seen prints made from the glass plate negatives, one can only imagine the impact when, for the first time in almost one hundred years, Glenn held in his hands the only photograph he had ever seen of his baby sister, who had died at the age of two. He and Nadine were overcome with emotion.

As we conclude the publication of this book in 2016, Glenn is 103 and Nadine is 96. In fact, it would not have been unreasonable to assume that Glenn was rapidly approaching his last days. Had that happened, the knowledge of the subjects of these beautiful family photographs would have been lost forever. Another chapter in our community's collective legacy would also have been irretrievable.

THE PUBLISHING TEAM

Steve Noll: Steve Noll has served as the executive director of the Jackson County Historical Society since 2004. A lifelong resident of the Kansas City area and a local history enthusiast since childhood, Steve has been associated with numerous local historic and civic organizations, and he has amassed a collection with hundreds of artifacts related to Kansas City's events, businesses, and local institutions. Having assisted others in producing local history books, this is Steve's attempt to share the area's past with others in the community.

A graduate of the University of Kansas, Steve has had a variety of occupational roles throughout his career, primarily in the fields of manufacturing and distribution. Steve and his wife, Marianne, have resided in Prairie Village since 1983, where he has served on the city council for more than twenty years.

Bruce Mathews: For more than 30 years, Bruce Mathews has been a commercial photographer based in Kansas City. His assignments have taken him throughout the continental United States, Hawaii, and Canada. Among his clients were the following: the Club Managers Association of America; the Golf Course Superintendents Association of America; the Harry S. Truman Library & Museum; Children's Mercy Hospital and Clinics; Tom Watson Design; and Washburn University.

Now retired from assignment photography, Bruce is engaged in photographing, writing, and publishing books about the history of Kansas City. *Kansas City: Our Collective Memories, Vol. 1*, represents a joint endeavor undertaken with noted historian Steve Noll. Previous works published and co-published by Bruce include the following award-winning books: *Elmwood Cemetery: Stories of Kansas City; The Kansas City Spirit: Stories of Service Above Self; Kansas City's Historic Union Cemetery: Lessons for the Future, from the Garden of Time; and Windows of Kansas City: As Art, History and Inspiration*. Bruce was a 2011 recipient of the Kansas City Spirit Award, given annually to individuals who have contributed to making Kansas City a better place in which to live.

Lynn Mackle: Lynn Mackle is a freelance writer and art historian. She curated a loan exhibition with an accompanying catalogue on the life and art of painter George Van Millett (1864-1953). She has written features for a variety of area publications, and she served as prose editor for Veterans' Voices, a national publication sponsored by the Hospitalized Veterans Writing Project.

Lynn was a contributing writer for *The Kansas City Spirit*, published in 2012 by Bruce Mathews thru Kansas City Star Books. She edited Bruce Mathews' *Windows of Kansas City: As Art, History and Inspiration*.

Lynn graduated from Mary Baldwin College with a degree in Spanish, spending a year in Madrid as an undergraduate. Returning to the academic arena, she earned master's degrees in both English and art history from the University of Missouri-Kansas City.

David Spaw: A native of the Kansas City area, David Spaw is a graphic designer and photographer. He and his wife, Sandy, are the parents of three sons, and they have two grandchildren. David has volunteered with the Boy Scouts of America, and he has been involved with his local homes association, as well as the Leawood Garden Club and the Mo-Kan Daylily Society. He is also active with his parish.

David was fortunate to spend six summers interning at Hallmark Cards, working in several departments related to graphic design, including photography, pre-press, printing, package design, and store planning. After completing military duty by serving in the U.S. Navy, he returned to Hallmark Cards and headed up a division of the marketing department in the role of art director.

David also worked at Lowell Press, designing numerous coffee table books. These works featured such noted Western American artists as Clark Hulings, Wilson Hurley, W. R. Leigh, R. Brownell McGrew, and sculptor Bob Scriver.

Of local interest, David worked on *Westport, Missouri's Port of Many Returns* by Patricia Cleary Miller; Kansas City, Missouri: *An Architectural History, 1826-1976*, by George Ehrlich; and *Colorado Treasures*, by James R. Hamil. Bruce Mathews' book, *Windows of Kansas City, As Art, History and Inspiration*, was among his latest design endeavors.

Kathy Barnard
: Kathy Barnard has been creating architectural art glass masterpieces since 1980. Locally, her commissions can be seen in the following locations: the Jewish Community Center in Overland Park, Kansas; the Temple of the Community of Christ Church in Independence, Mo.; the Midland Theatre in downtown Kansas City; the Ozark National Life Building at Ninth and Locust; and many other public and private settings. Kathy has also completed commissions in such distant locales as Apia, Samoa, and Taunusstein, Germany.

Kathy is a 1977 graduate of the University of Kansas, with a B.F.A. degree in graphic art and illustration. She is a member of the American Glass Guild. From 2015 to 2017, she served as president of the Stained Glass Association of America. Kathy has received numerous local and national awards; in 1991, she was inducted into the Women's Hall of Fame at the University of Kansas.

For more information about the artist's works go to www.kathybarnardstudio.com.

Doug Weaver
: Doug Weaver is a journalist and book publisher. He has produced more than 350 book titles in his career, on topics ranging from regional history to entertainment, art, architecture, travel, crime, and the craft of quilting.

Doug is now a partner and the business manager of Mission Point Press, a book publisher based in Traverse City, Michigan, which has published this book. Doug owns Chandler Lake Books, also based in Traverse City.

Doug holds a master's degree in business administration from Rockhurst University in Kansas City, and a bachelor's degree in journalism from the University of Illinois.

Doug was the business editor at the Springfield (Illinois) Journal-Register, editor of Corporate Report Wisconsin, and the business editor at The Kansas City Star. In 2000, The Kansas City Star named him Manager of Strategic Business Development to develop niche revenue opportunities for the newspaper, including book publishing and retailing.

In 2004, Doug was named publisher of Kansas City Star Books, the newspaper's book-publishing division. Prior to the sale of that operation in 2015, Star Books operated three imprints under Doug's direction: Kansas City Star Books, Kansas City Star Quilts, and Rockhill Books.

Mission Point Press and Chandler Lake Books were formed shortly after the sale of Kansas City Star Books.

Walsworth Publishing Company
: Walsworth, among the top ten book printers in the United States, is headquartered in Marceline, Missouri, a town commonly known as the boyhood home of Walt Disney.

In 1937, Don Walsworth settled in Marceline to print playbills with a borrowed typewriter and a mimeograph machine. The product line was soon expanded to include cookbooks. Following World War II, memorial books to honor those who had served their country were added.

In 1947, Walsworth began to produce yearbooks. In 1970, the commercial printing division was established to balance the cyclical yearbook production schedule, adding textbooks, catalogs, magazines, and other specialty publications to the Walsworth line.

Today, Walsworth remains a family-owned company that employs more than 1,250 people worldwide. More than 250 Walsworth employees have given at least twenty years of service to the company. Several members of various families work for Walsworth; at times, three generations have been employed simultaneously. The company boasts more than 675 employees who have attained the prestigious Master Printer of America status.

BIBLIOGRAPHY

The 1900 Democratic National Convention. Clipping file. Missouri Valley Special Collections, Kansas City Public Library, Kansas City, MO.

"The 1900 Democratic National Convention." *Wikipedia*. Last modified June 30, 2016. Accessed July 20, 2016. https://en.wikipedia.org/wiki/1900_Democratic_National_Convention.

The 1928 Republican National Convention. Clipping file. Missouri Valley Special Collections, Kansas City Public Library, Kansas City, MO.

"The 1928 Republican National Convention." *Wikipedia*. Last modified June 29, 2016. Accessed July 20, 2016. https://en.wikipedia.org/wiki/1928_Republican_National_Convention.

Aber, Sarah Jane Sandusky. "An Architectural History of the Liberty Memorial in Kansas City, Missouri, 1918–1935." Master's thesis, University of Missouri–Kansas City, 1988.

"An Old Timer Sadly Recalls Gay Days of Tap Room Fame." *Kansas City Journal*, June 4, 1928.

Bauske, Clay (museum curator, Harry S. Truman Library and Museum). Interview by the author, March 2016.

Bernstein, Bob. Interview by the author, February 2016.

Bettinger, Bruce. Interview by the author, February 2016.

Bresee, Col. Howard F., Director, American Prisoner of War Information, letter to Mr. Frederic H. Olander Sr., April 3, 1945. In possession of Mina Steen.

"Bullene, Moore, Emery & Co. Shopping Guide." Missouri Valley Special Collections, Kansas City Public Library, Kansas City, MO, August 20, 1891.

Bush, Frances. "First Librarian Foresaw City's Growth." *Kansas City Star*, July 18, 1978.

Bushnell, Michael. "Postcards of Historic Northeast: Baltimore Hotel Stunned around the Turn of the Century." *Northeast News*, February 17, 2010.

Bushnell, Michael. "Postcards of Historic Northeast: Upscale Baltimore Hotel Hosted Presidents." *Northeast News*, February 18, 2009.

"Carrie Westlake Whitney." *Kansas City Journal*, November 14, 1903.

"Carrie Westlake Whitney." *Kansas City Star*, April 9, 1934.

Chaurand, Enrique A. "Los Indios…A Family Affair: Playing Ball is a Way of Life." *Kansas City Star*, August 16, 1996.

Chávez Ortíz, Genovevo Teodoro. "Pitch'm Fast Pauly: The Mexican-American Fast-Pitch Softball Leagues." *Latino Baseball History Project Newsletter*, November 2015, 2–3.

Chávez, Gene T. Interview by the author, February 2016.

"The City Union Mission." *In God's Human Sparrows*, edited by Carla Cosgrove and Angela Torres, 3–7. Kansas City, MO: City Union Mission, 2004.

Coleman, Daniel. "Jay B. Dillingham: Businessman, 1910–2007." Missouri Valley Special Collections, Kansas City Public Library, Kansas City, MO, 2009.

Coolidge, Calvin. "Address at the Dedication of the Liberty Memorial at Kansas City, Missouri." November 11, 1926. Online by Gerhard Peters and John T. Woolley, *The American Presidency Project*. Accessed July 20, 2016. http://www.presidency.ucsb.edu/ws/?pid=413.

Davies, R. E. G. *Airlines of the United States Since 1914*. Washington, DC: Smithsonian Institution Press, 1982.

Davies, R. E. G. *TWA: An Airline and Its Aircraft*. Illustrated by Mike Machat. N.p.: Paladwr Press, 2001.

DeAngelo, Dory, and Jane Fifield Flynn. Kansas City Style. Kansas City, MO: Harrow Books, 1990.

DeAngelo, Dory. "Kansas City History: Thirsty Crowd Used 'Highball Alley' Tunnel." *Kansas City Star*, April 19, 1989.

"The Death of Carrie Westlake Whitney." *Kansas City Times*, April 9, 1934.

Dillingham, John. Interview by the author, 2015–2016.

DiSalvo, Daniel, Jr. Interview by the author, 2014–2016.

Donovan, Derek. *Lest the Ages Forget: Kansas City's Liberty Memorial*. Kansas City, MO: Kansas City Star Books, 2013.

Doty, Dan. Interview by the author, 2016.

Dunlop, Acting Adjutant General, telegram to Frederic H. Olander Sr., December 21, 1944.

"EBT Long a Part of Downtown Scene." *Kansas City Star*, February 11, 1971.

Emert, Carol, and Dick Rees (volunteers at the TWA Museum). Interview by the author, December 2015.

Emery, Bird and Thayer Building, National Register of Historic Places Inventory Nomination Form. Prepared by M. Patricia Holmes and Shelia M. Hannah. Missouri State Park Board and Historical Survey and Planning Office, Jefferson City, MO, November 12, 1971.

Encyclopædia Britannica Online, s. v. "United States Presidential Election of 1928." Last modified March 14, 2016. Accessed July 20, 2016. https://www.britannica.com/event/United-States-presidential-election-of-1928.

Ferruzza, Charles. "A Century of Meatless Eating in Kansas City." *Pitch Weekly*, May 11, 2012.

Ferruzza, Charles. "Ralph Gaines: Remembering a Legendary Restaurateur (1918–1979)." *Pitch Weekly*, November 20, 2013.

Finley, Nancy. *Finley Ball: How Two Baseball Outsiders Turned the Oakland A's into a Dynasty and Changed the Game Forever.* Washington, DC: Regnery History, 2016.

Ford, Susan Jezak. "James Greenwood: School Superintendent, 1837–1914." Missouri Valley Special Collections, Kansas City Public Library, Kansas City, MO, 2003.

Foster, Neal (EBT Collector). Interview by the author, June 2015.

Fowler, Richard B. *Leaders in Our Town*. Kansas City, MO: Burd & Fletcher, 1952.

Francis, Donna. "Baltimore Hotel." Missouri Valley Special Collections, Kansas City Public Library, Kansas City, MO, 1999.

"Frederic H. Olander Jr." Obituary. *Kansas City Star*, January 31, 2002.

"Golden Ox." *Wikipedia*. Last modified May 3, 2016. Accessed July 20, 2016. https://en.wikipedia.org/wiki/Golden_Ox.

Gould, Sam. Interview by the author, 2013.

Helzberg, Barnett. Interview by the author.

Hendricks, Mike. "The Golden Ox: Steak and Tradition." *Kansas City Star*, November 15, 1990.

Herrold, Benjamin. "Memories of Old Stockyards Remain." *Missouri Farmer Today*, October 24, 2012.

"Historic Aircraft's Design Still Brings Applause." *Kansas City Star*, January 27, 1976.

Hoffman, William H., Edward O. Swovelan, and Jerry Ackerman. *Kansas City, Missouri Public Library 1873–1973, an Illustrated History.* N.p., 1973.

Hughes, Mamie, and Bob Kendrick (Negro Leagues Baseball Museum). Interview, January 2016.

Kansas City Public Library. *One Hundred Twenty-five Years of Serving You: Kansas City Public Library*. Brochure. Kansas City, MO: 1998.

Kansas City Times. *Kansas City: Its Resources and Their Development—A Souvenir of the Kansas City Times*. Kansas City, MO: Interstate Publishing Company, 1890.

Kennedy, Robert C. "On This Day: July 4, 1900." HarpWeek. https://www.nytimes.com/learning/general/onthisday/harp/0704.html.

Kansas City Public Library. *Key Events in the History of the Kansas City Public Library 1873–1993*. Pamphlet. Kansas City, MO: 1999.

Kirk, Charlotte. Interview by the author, April 2016.

Krigel, Gayle. Interview by the author, March 2016.

Kubis, Glenn, and Nadine Kubis. Interview by the author, April 2013.

Lewandowski, Zack. "How Mexican-Americans in Kansas Built a Community Around Softball." KCUR 89.3. Broadcast July 9, 2013. http://kcur.org/post/how-mexican-americans-kansas-built-community-around-softball.

Liberty Memorial, National Register of Historic Places Nomination Form. Prepared by Cydney E. Millstein. Kansas City, MO, Parks and Recreation Department, April 3, 2000.

Liebling, Beth. Interview by the author, 2016.

Londré, Felicia. Interview by the author, 2016.

Loose, Jacob and Ella, Archives. Greater Kansas City Community Foundation, Kansas City, MO.

Magerl, Barbara. "Carrie Westlake Whitney: Librarian and Director of the Kansas City Public Library." Missouri Valley Special Collections, Kansas City Public Library, Kansas City, MO, 1999.

McFerrin, Ann. "Liberty Memorial, Penn Valley Park." Missouri Valley Special Collections, Kansas City Public Library, Kansas City, MO, 1926.

Miller Center of Public Affairs, University of Virginia. "Herbert Hoover: Campaigns and Elections." Accessed July 20, 2016. http://millercenter.org¬/president/biography/hoover-campaigns-and-elections.

"Miracle at MCI." *Independence Examiner,* January 26, 1976.

Montgomery, Rick, and Shirl Kasper. Kansas City: *An American Story.* Kansas City, MO: Kansas City Star Books, 1999.

Morales, Jerry, and Tony Morales. Interview by the author, June 2016.

Morrison, Denise, and Anna Marie Tutera. Interview by the author, Kansas City Museum, April 2016.

Newill, Cody. "A Look Back at the Three Times Kansas City Hosted National Political Conventions." KCUR 89.3. June 11, 2014. http://kcur.org/post/look-back-3-times-kansas-city-hosted-national-political-conventions.

Nichols, Miller. Special Bulletin to all Personnel, J.C. Nichols Real Estate Company, July 1, 1963. In possession of Sally Ruddy.

Nofsinger, Roland. Interview by the author, 2014.

Olander, Lt. Fred H., Jr. *My Kriegie Days.* POW diary. In possession of Mina Steen.

"The Owl Drug Company." *Wikipedia.* Last modified February 27, 2016. Accessed July 20, 2016. https://en.wikipedia.org/wiki/The_Owl_Drug_Company.

Parton, Nancy. Interview by the author, 2016.

Pistilli, Kevin (Raphael Hotel Group). Interview by the author, May 2016.

Priests of Pallas. Vertical file, Missouri Valley Special Collections, Kansas City Public Library, Kansas City, MO.

Ray, Mrs. Sam. "Post Card From Old Kansas City: Hotel Baltimore . . . Grand in Its Day." *Kansas City Star.*

Rees, Richard D. Interview by the author.

Roe, Jason. "Gettysburg of the West." *This Week in Kansas City History.* Kansas City Public Library, Kansas City, MO. http://www.kclibrary.org/blog/week-kansas-city-history/gettysburg-west.

Ruddy, Sally Lee Kaney Tourtellot. Personal journal. In private collection.

Ruddy, Sally. Interview by the author, 2013–2016.

Ruchay, Sam (supervisory archivist, Harry S. Truman Library and Museum). Interview by the author, March 2016.

Saathoff, Ken. Interview by the author, 2016.

Saathoff, Ken. Loose Mansion. Informational flyer. Kansas City, MO: Loose Mansion, 2012.

Santillán, Richard. "Mexican Baseball Teams in the Midwest, 1916–1965: The Politics of Cultural Survival and Civil Rights." *Perspectives in Mexican-American Studies* 7 (2001): 131–51.

Seguí, Diego. Interview by the author, June 16, 2016.

Siddiqi, Asif. "Trans World Airlines." *U.S. Centennial of Flight Commission.* http://www.centennialofflight.net/essay/Commercial_Aviation/TWA/Tran14.htm.

Smith, Joyce. "Economy Brings End to Golden Ox." *Kansas City Star*, November 11, 2003.

Starbuck, Dave (Kansas City Baseball Historical Society). Interview by the author, May 2016.

Steen, Mina. Interview by the author, April 2016.

Taylor, Tom. Interview by the author, 2016.

Taylor, Tom. *Unity Village.* Charleston, SC: Arcadia Publishing, 2009.

Toma, George (groundskeeper). Interview by the author, January 2016.

"Trans World Airlines." *Wikipedia.* Last modified May 10, 2016. Accessed July 20, 2016. https://en.wikipedia.org/wiki/Trans_World_Airlines.

Trans World Airlines Executive Council. TWA: *A Pictorial History.* N.p.: privately printed, 1981.

Ulio, J. A., Adjutant General, telegram to Frederic H. Olander Sr., May 29, 1945.

Vanderberg-Rohlfing, Julianna. *I Never Asked for the Easy Way: The People Who Helped Shape City Union Mission.* Kansas City, MO: City Union Mission Publishing, 1999.

Vedros, Nick, and Patty Vedros. Interview by the author, 2016.

Westport Historical Society. *The Harris-Kearney House.* Pamphlet. Kansas City, MO.

Westport Historical Society Archives. Kansas City, MO.

INDEX

Acme Brass Custom Plating: 23

Acme Brass Machine Works: 23

Aladdin Hotel: 68

Allis, Barney: 59, 64, 68

Alpha Project: 47-49

American Biscuit Company: 28

American Legion Post #213: 120

American Royal: 12, 25, 66, 72, 77, 79, 133, 153, 200

Andrews, Theresa: 18

Armour & Company: 201-202

Barstow School: 204

Bartle, Mayor H. Roe: 23-25, 93, 106, 199

Battle of Westport: 9, 10, 191

Bauske, Clay: 182

Beach, Mayor Albert: 88

Bennett, Philomene: 206-207

Berkley, Mayor Richard L.: 128

Bernstein, Bob: 80-81

Bernstein-Rein Advertising: 80-81

Bettinger, Bruce: 21-22

Bikales, Gina: 203

Bingham, George Caleb: 186-187

Bird, Annie: 36

Bird, Joseph Taylor: 36

Bishop, Frances A.: 167

Bishop, Mel: 203-204

Blues Stadium: 102, 108

Blunt, Sen. Roy: 98

Boone, Albert Gallatin: 6

BOTAR: 66

Boy Scouts – Greater Kansas City Area Council: 23

Branton, Mary Shaw "Shawsie": 181

Brett, George: 102

Brooks, Chester Claude: 214

Brooks, Lillian Spangler: 214

Bulkley, Beulah: 159-161

Bulkley, Rev. David: 159-163

Bullene, Moore & Emery: 35

Bullene, Thomas: 35-36

Bushnell, Michael: 11, 13, 15, 59

Byram's Ford: 9

Calvary Baptist Church: 191

Canfield, Anne: 134

Ceceña, Tony Jr.: 120

Chambers, Annie: 163

Charles B. Wheeler Downtown Airport: 13, 41-43, 46, 48, 49

Charlie-O, the mule: 109

Chaurand, Enrique: 118, 120, 122

Chávez, Gene: 120-121

Children's Fountain: 14

Children's Mercy Hospital: 32, 105

Chouteau, François Gesseau: 3

Chouteau, Bérénice Thérèse Ménard: 3

City Market: 19

City Union Mission: 158-160, 162-163

Cleaver, Rep. Emanuel: 98

Coates, Kersey: 4, 35

Coates – Kersey Coates Drive: 4

Coates & Bullene: 35

Coates & Gillis: 35

Cohen, Rabbi Herman M.: 143

Coleman, Daniel: 77

Colmery, Harry W.: 150

Colony Steak House: 76

Combs, Irwin: 99

Commerce Trust Company: 14-15

Commercial Club: 21

Compton, Dorothea: 20

Compton, Louis: 20

Convention Hall, first: 11, 139

Convention Hall, second: 140-142

Corbin, Tom: 14

Corie Cracker and Confectionery Company: 28

Corrigan, Bernard: 52, 59

Country Club Plaza: 9, 27, 59, 198, 202, 215

Cowgill, Mayor James: 83

Crown Center: 203

Curtiss, Louis: 50-53

Daily Drovers Telegram: 20

Daniel, Clifton Truman: 181

Darby, Sen. Harry: 78

DeCoursey Creamery Company: 16

DeCoursey, James H.: 16

Deramus, Bill: 200

DiCapo, Carl: 128

Dillingham, Frances Thompson: 71

Dillingham, Jay: 25, 71, 74, 76-79, 199, 200

Dillingham, John: 25, 77, 185, 200

DiPardo, Tony: 106

DiRenna, James A.: 128

DiSalvo, Daniel Jr.: 154-157

DiSalvo, Pvt. Daniel Sr.: 154-157

Disney, Walt: 171

Dobbs, Gloria: 4, 15, 37, 139, 181

Dole, Sen. Robert: 145-146

Doty, Dan: 160, 162

Duncan, David Douglas: 207

EBT Restaurant: 39

Elms Hotel: 69

Elmwood Cemetery: 117, 181

Emery, Bird, Thayer Dry Goods Company: 34-39

Emery, W. E.: 35

Ewing, George: 6

Ewing, William: 6

Fairfax Airport: 45

Faxon & Gallagher Drug Company: 21-22

Faxon, Frank: 21

Ferruzza, Charles: 17

Fillmore, Charles: 17

Fillmore, Myrtle: 17

Finley, Charles O.: 108-109, 111, 115, 125, 180

Finley, Nancy: 115

First National Bank: 173, 191

Foster, Neal: 34-35, 37

Future Farmers of America (FFA): 76

Gaines, Ralph: 76

Gallagher, John A.: 21

Garver, Ned: 113

Gilbert, Joe: 76

Gilbert/Robinson Company: 76

Gillis, William: 35

Golden Ox Restaurant: 70-79

Gorman, Anita: 7, 10, 13, 14, 95-97, 145

Goslin, Charles: 6

Graves, Rep. Sam: 98

Greater Kansas City Chamber of Commerce: 79, 107, 199

Greater Kansas City Golden Glove: 126-131

Gregory, Vern and Frances: 129

Greenwood, James M.: 164-165, 167-168

Greer, Steve: 76

Guadalupe Centers, Inc.: 119, 123

Haff, Capt. Carroll Barse: 99

Hale, Donald R.: 136

Hall, Joyce C.: 47, 85, 93-94

Hall, Porter T.: 36

Hallmark Cards: 24, 47, 85, 115

Hannibal & St. Joseph Railway: 209

Hannibal Bridge: 209

Happy Meal, The: 80-81

Harris-Kearney House: 5, 210-211

Harris House Hotel: 5, 209

Harris, Rev. Elton: 88

Harris, Col. John: 5

Harris, Henrietta Simpson: 5

Harvey the Rabbit: 101, 109, 116

Heim, Joseph: 117

Helzberg Diamonds: 16

Helzberg, Barnett: 16

Helzberg, Shirley Bush: 16

Herbst, John: 135-137

Hernandez, Paul "Pauly": 120, 122

Hess, Dr. H. Lewis: 99

Hockaday, James K. B.: 99

Holmes, Nancy Tyler: 181

Horton, James: 21

Hotel Baltimore: 50-59

Hotel Muehlebach: 59, 60-69

Howser, Dick: 110

Hummel, August: 23

Hunt, Lamar: 23, 114

Hunter, Jim "Catfish": 111

Ice, Frances: 43, 46

Independence Bottling Company: 21

Irwin, Lambdin E.: 133

Jackson County Agricultural and Mechanical Association: 191

Jackson County Courthouse: 19

Jackson County Historical Society: 6, 67, 99, 134-135, 137

Jackson, George Washington: 201

Jesse, Randall: 78

Johnson, Arnold: 108

Johnson, Dot: 4

Johnson, Sarah Davis: 187

Johnson, Rev. Thomas: 187

Joyce, Dick: 111

Kanaga, Clinton W.: 24

Kanaga, Nina: 24

Kaney, Cliff: 197, 199, 200, 204

Kaney, Margaret "Polly": 197

Kansas, University of: 24, 149, 203

Kansas City Area Transportation Authority: 24

Kansas City Art Institute: 24

Kansas City Athletics: 108-117, 123, 179, 180

Kansas City Blues: (baseball): 101-104, 179

Kansas City Blues, (football): 117

Kansas City Board of Education: 21, 165, 167, 171

Kansas City Bond & Mortgage Company: 177

Kansas City Cable Company: 169

Kansas City Chiefs: 23, 114-115, 117

Kansas City Connecting Railroad Company: 71

Kansas City Country Club: 32

Kansas City Cowboys (baseball): 117, 119

Kansas City Cowboys (football): 117

Kansas City International Airport: 13, 45, 49, 79

Kansas City Journal: 167, 211

Kansas City Live Stock Exchange: 149, 199

Kansas City Live Stock Exchange Building: 71-72, 74, 78, 149

Kansas City Monarchs: 104-105, 111, 120

Kansas City Museum: 19, 121, 178, 196, 209, 211

Kansas City Public Library: 2, 7, 17, 20-22, 30, 32, 36, 50, 53, 58, 62, 74, 88, 104, 108, 119, 139-142, 144, 164-173, 201, 214

Kansas City Royals: 107, 110, 114-115, 119

Kansas City Southern Railway: 200

Kansas City Spirit: 47-48, 79, 83, 85, 95, 106, 139, 144

Kansas City Star: 74, 78-79, 86, 112, 117-118, 120, 122, 124-125, 127-128, 131, 133, 167

Kansas City Stockyards: 20, 71-72, 78, 199, 200

Kansas City Stockyards Company: 25, 71

Kansas City T-Bones: 119

Kansas City Toy and Miniature Museum: 204

Kansas City Zoo: 5, 7

Kansas City, Kansas, Chamber of Commerce: 79

Kansas City, Missouri, Aviation Department: 13

Kansas City, Missouri, Board of Police Commissioners: 24

Kansas City, Missouri, Centennial: 11-12, 15

Kansas City, Missouri, City Hall: 19

Kansas City, Missouri, Parks and Recreation Department: 96

Kansas City's National Political Conventions: 138-147

Kasper, Shirl: 133

Kauffman Stadium: 119

Kearney, Col. Charles E.: 5, 209-210

Kearney, Hattie Drisdom: 208-211

Kearney, Josephine Harris: 5-6, 209-210

Kemper Arena: 76, 131, 144-147

Kemper, James M.: 68, 84

Kemper, Rufus Crosby: 84

Keneseth Israel-Beth Shalom, Congregation: 143

Kessler, George: 84

Kirk, Charlotte Wornall and Stephen: 187-191

Klice, Bubble: 128

Krigel, Bruce: 192-195

Krigel, Gayle: 192-195

Kubis, Bernice Lela: 212, 215

Kubis, Glenn: 212-215

Kubis: Lela Edna Spangler: 213, 214

Kubis, Maxine Gertrude: 212-215

Kubis, Nadine: 212-215

Kubis, Robert E.: 214

Latino Baseball: 118-125

Latino baseball teams: Aztecas - 118, 120-121, 125; Bravos – 122, 123; Eagles – 120-121; Locos – 121; Pirates – 121; Railway Ice Co. - 121

Liberty Memorial: 3-5, 66, 82-99

Liberty Memorial Association: 83, 87, 88

Lillis, Bishop Thomas F.: 143

Little Blowhard: 109

Londré, Felicia: 52, 133-137

Long, Robert Alexander: 84, 87-89

Loose Brothers Manufacturing Company: 28

Loose Mansion: 27-28, 30, 31

Loose Park: 9, 10, 27, 32-33

Loose, Ella Anna Clark: 27-28, 32-33, 84

Loose, Jacob L.: 27-28, 32-33, 84

Loose, Joseph S.: 28, 32

Loose-Wiles Biscuit Company: 28-30

Lovejoy, Madame: 163

Lyric Opera: 203

Lykins Neighborhood Association: 117

Magonigle, H. Van Buren: 84

Maris, Roger: 110

Marriott Kansas City Downtown Hotel: 68

Martin, John: 106, 115

Mathews, Bruce: 1, 11, 50, 100, 124, 181, 184, 208, 213

Mathews, Charlie: 100

Mathews, O.K.: 100

McCaskill, Sen. Claire: 98

McGuire, Dr. Clarence: 99

McHughes, Tom: 128

McKim, Americus V.: 117

McNally Park: 122

Mehl, Ernie: 128

Methodist Episcopal Diocese of Kansas City: 143

Meyer, Lt. Walter H.: 99

Mid-Continent International Airport: 13, 45, 79

Miller, Patricia Cleary: 55-57

Millstein, Cydney E.: 96

Miracle Pictures: 198

Missouri Valley Special Collections: 2, 7, 17, 20-22, 30, 32, 36, 50, 53, 58, 62, 74, 77, 88, 104, 108, 139-142, 144, 166-167, 170-171, 173, 201, 214

Montgall, Capt. Rufus: 99

Montgomery, Rick: 133

Morales family: 126-131

Morales, Jerry: 126-131

Morales, Mark: 127

Muehlebach Beer Company: 101

Muehlebach Field: 101-102, 104

Muehlebach, George: 61

Muehlebach, George E.: 61, 101

Municipal Airport: 4-5, 13, 41, 44, 46, 79, 181

Municipal Auditorium: 5, 144

Municipal Stadium: 100-117

Murphy, Bill and Jeri: 178

Murphy, Mike: 128

Myers, Charlie: 128

National Biscuit Company: 28

National World War I Museum and Memorial: 98

National World War I Museum: 85-86, 89, 90-91, 94, 96-99

Nau, Rev. Carl W.: 151

Naylor, Dr. Matthew: 98

Neff, Jay Holcomb: 20

Nelly Don: 12

Nelson, William Rockhill: 172

Nelson-Atkins Museum of Art: 24, 172

Nichols, J. C.: 59, 84, 88, 197-198

Nichols - J. C. Nichols Company: 197, 202

Nichols – J. C. Nichols Fountain: 3

Nichols, Miller: 202

Nichols, Mrs. J. C.: 99

Noel, Jim: 183

Nofsinger, Rowland: 208, 211

Noll, Steve: 2-3, 5-6, 11, 12, 17, 19-20, 30, 35, 46, 51, 61, 63-65, 70-71, 73-76, 137, 140, 176

Norman, William O.: 177-179

O'Brien, Karol: 23, 82

Odom, Johnny "Blue Moon": 111, 113

O'Hara, Jack: 24

O'Keefe, Jim: 137

Olander, John: 149

Olander, Frederic Herbert, Sr.: 149

Olander, Lt. Frederic Herbert, Jr: 148-153

Olander, Mary Colmery: 149, 150

O'Neil, John J. "Buck": 104, 106, 107

Paige, Satchel: 104, 111-112, 124, 125

Partain, Dorri: 114

Parton, Nancy: 27, 28

Partridge, Bishop S. C: 143

Pembroke School: 204

Pendergast, Thomas J.: 22

Petticoat Lane: 35-36

Penn Valley Park: 5

Pickwick Hotel: 176

Pickwick Papers: 176

Pioneer Mother Memorial: 4, 5

Pistilli, Kevin: 68

Pistilli, Philip: 68

Polly's Soda Pop: 20, 21

Priests of Pallas: 132-137

Prince, Eva: 163

Radisson Muehlebach: 68

Raphael Hotel Group: 63, 64, 68

Rauschelbach, Bill: 76

Rauschelbach, Jerry: 76

Rees, Dick: 20, 40, 67, 146-147, 202

Rees, Janet: 146-147

Reeves, Dr. E. A.: 161

Reicher, Nancy and Philip: 63

Reyes, Steve: 118

Richardson, Hayes: 128

Richardson, Dr. Katharine Berry: 105

Roberts, Dwight: 199

Robinson, Paul: 76

Rockhurst High School: 204

Rosier, Philippe de: 198, 204

Rowe, Douglas: 41

Rowland, Landon: 200

Rowland, Sarah: 200, 204

Ruddy, John: 197

Ruddy, Sally Lee Kaney Tourtellot: 196-207

Ruppert Stadium: 100-102

Saathoff, Barbara: 26, 28-29

Saathoff, Ken: 26, 28-29

Saddle and Sirloin Club: 12

Saint Luke's Hospital: 153

Salas, Frank: 118

Sanders – Coon Sanders Nighthawks: 66
Santillán, Richard: 120, 125
Scotty: 160
Scout – The Scout Statue: 4, 5
Sebree, Frank: 84, 88
Seguí, David: 123
Seguí, Diego: 112, 123-125
Seguí, Emily Sauceda: 123-124
Shawnee Methodist Mission: 187
Sheidley Cattle Company: 169
Sheidley, George: 168-169
Shawnee Park: 122
Siebern, Norm: 113
Smart, Chris: 94
Smart, David Oliver III: 196
Smart, Margaret E. "Peggy" Tourtellot: 196
Smith, Charles Ashley: 165, 172
Smith, Laura Conyers: 33
Smith, William Joseph "Cable Car": 134
Society for the Preservation and Encouragement of Barber Shop Quartet Singing in America (SPEBSQSA): 66
Southern Belle: 200, 201
Southwest High School: 149, 204
Spangler, A. J.: 214
Spangler, Mae: 214
Sprint Arena: 76
St. Charles Borromeo Parish Church: 206
St. Paul's Episcopal Church: 151
Steen, Mina: 148-153
Starbuck, Bill: 113
Starbuck, Dave: 103, 109-113, 117
Strauss-Peyton Studio: 67, 99, 105
Sunset Hill School: 204
Sunshine Biscuit Company: 29, 30

Swift and Henry Livestock Commission Company: 199
Swope Park: 4, 7-9
Swope, Col. Thomas H.: 7-8, 172
Tartabull, Jose: 113
Taylor, Tom: 8, 17, 43-44, 46, 54, 60, 65, 135, 137, 176, 202
Teel, Bill: 76

Tempel, Abigail & Fred: 54-55
Tension Envelope Corporation: 105
Thayer, William Bridges: 36
The Pitch: 17
Thomas, Gertrude Spangler: 214
Thomas, Roy S.: 214
Throneberry, Marvin E. "Marvelous Marv": 112
Toma, George: 116
Tompkins, Ron: 111
Tourtellot, Dallas: 201
Tourtellot, George W. Sr.: 201-202
Tourtellot, George W. Jr.: 196, 202
Tourtellot, George W. III: 196-198, 207
Tourtellot, Margaret "Madge" Topping: 196
Tourtellot, Mary Ann Stephens: 201
Tourtellot, Paris: 201
Trans World Airlines: 13, 18, 40-49
Trianon Hotel Company: 68
Truman, Bess Wallace: 175, 179-180, 182-183
Truman - Bess Truman's Bridge Club: Mary G. Shaw, Linda King, Natalie Ott Wallace, Helena F. Crowe, Mag Barkley Noel, Edna Hutchinson, Adelaide Twyman, Thelma Pallette, Lucy Peters, May Wallace: 183
Truman Home: 5
Truman, Harry S.: 66-67, 69, 79, 93-94, 108, 128, 141, 143, 174-185, 206
Truman – Harry S. Truman Library and Museum: 5, 69, 94, 108, 138, 141, 143, 174-185
Truman – Harry S. Truman Sports Complex: 114, 119
Truman, Margaret: 181-182
TWA Museum: 41-43, 46, 48-49
Union Cemetery: 208, 210-211
Union Station: 3-5, 83-84, 203, 205
Unity Vegetarian Inn and Cafeteria: 17
Unity Village: 17, 204
Valentine-Radford Advertising Agency: 24
Van Brunt, Henry: 36, 51
Van Brunt & Howe Architects: 36
Vanderberg, Rev. Maurice: 162

Vanderberg-Rholfing, Juliana: 158
Vedros, Nick: 16, 45
Vedros, Patty: 16
Volker, William: 5, 84
Waldorf, Bishop E. L.: 143
Wampler, Lillian Spangler Brooks: 214
Watson, Marshall: 203
Watson, Tom: 102, 107
WDAF: 66, 78
Weeks, Mrs. Phil K.: 132
Western Gallery of Art: 172
Westport Historical Society: 5-6, 10, 210
Wheeler, Mayor Charles B.: 128
Whitfield, Jim: 117
Whitney, Carrie Westlake: 164-167, 171
Wilborn, Chris: 15, 44, 72, 78, 84, 86, 91, 101-102, 104, 107, 110, 112, 147
William Jewell College: 191
Willis Wood Theatre: 52, 59, 66
Wood, Col. Willis: 52
Woods, Dr. William Stone: 14
Wornall, Charles Hardin: 191
Wornall, Edna: 191
Wornall, Eliza Johnson: 186-191
Wornall, Fannie: 191
Wornall, Francis Clay: 191
Wornall, John B.: 186-191
Wornall, John B. Jr.: 191
Wornall, John B. IV: 186, 190
Wornall, Judith Ann Glover: 187
Wornall, Julia Kearney: 210-211
Wornall, Matilda Polk(e): 191
Wornall, Richard: 187
Wornall, Roma Johnson: 191
Wornall, Sallie: 191
Wornall, Thomas Johnson: 191
Yoder, Rep. Kevin: 98